M000230913

OKS IN THE LEADERS IN ACTION SERIES

A Place to Stand:
Vord of God in the Life of **Martin Luther**
Gene E. Veith

All Things for Good:
Steadfast Fidelity of **Stonewall Jackson**
J. Steven Wilkins

Beyond Stateliest Marble:
ssionate Femininity of **Anne Bradstreet**
by Douglas Wilson

uty: The Sterling Nobility of **Robert E. Lee**
by J. Steven Wilkins

The Uncommon Heroism of **Theodore Roosevelt**
by George Grant

Covenant: The Stalwart Courage of **John Knox**
by Douglas Wilson

g Father: The Heroic Legacy of **George Whitefield**
by Stephen Mansfield

Give Me Liberty:
promising Statesmanship of **Patrick Henry**
by David J. Vaughan

e Extraordinary Character of **Winston Churchill**
by Stephen Mansfield

Lion: The Spiritual Legacy of **C. S. Lewis**
by Terry W. Glaspey

The Pillars of Leadership
by David J. Vaughan

t: The Principled Politics of **William Wilberforce**
by David Vaughan

The Liberating Wisdom of **Booker T. Washington**
by Stephen Mansfield

OTHER BC

The

The

The F

Call of I

Carry a Big Stick

For Kirk and

Forgotten Foundi

The Uncon

Never Give In: T

Not a Tam

Statesman and Sa

Then Darkness Fle

g

Glory and Honor

THE MUSICAL AND ARTISTIC LEGACY OF JOHANN SEBASTIAN BACH

LEADERS
IN
ACTION

GREGORY WILBUR

DAVID VAUGHAN, GENERAL EDITOR

CUMBERLAND HOUSE

NASHVILLE, TENNESSEE

GLORY AND HONOR
PUBLISHED BY CUMBERLAND HOUSE PUBLISHING, INC.
431 Harding Industrial Drive
Nashville, Tennessee 37211

Copyright © 2005 by Gregory Wilbur

All rights reserved. No part of this book may be reproduced or transmit-
ted in any form or by any means, electronic or mechanical, including
photocopying and recording, or by any information storage and retrieval
system, without permission in writing from the publisher, except for
brief quotations in critical reviews and articles.

Unless otherwise indicated, all Scripture quotations are taken from The
Holy Bible, English Standard Version, copyright © 2001 by Crossway
Bibles, a division of Good News Publishers. Used by permission. All
rights reserved. Scripture quotations marked NEB are taken from the
New English Bible. © The Delegates of the Oxford University Press and
The Syndics of the Cambridge University Press 1961, 1970. Reprinted
by permission. Scripture quotations marked NKJV are taken from the
New King James Version. Copyright © 1979, 1980, 1982, Thomas Nel-
son, Inc., Publishers.

Cover design by Gore Studio, Inc., Nashville, Tennessee

Library of Congress Cataloging-in-Publication Data

Wilbur, Gregory, 1968–
  Glory and honor : the musical and artistic legacy of Johann
Sebastian Bach / Gregory Wilbur.
       p. cm. — (Leaders in action)
  Includes bibliographical references (p.) and index.
  ISBN-13: 978-1-58182-470-4 (hardcover : alk. paper)
  ISBN-10: 1-58182-470-X (hardcover : alk. paper)
  1. Bach, Johann Sebastian, 1685–1750. 2. Composers—
Germany—Biography. I. Title. II. Leaders in action series.
ML410.B1W53 2005
780.92—dc22   2005026003

Printed in the United States of America
1 2 3 4 5 6—09 08 07 06 05

To Nana,
for your love of music, of Bach, and me
and
To Eleanor,
may you continue your love of Bach
and may you share the same passions.
I love you, Little One.

CONTENTS

Foreword   xi

Acknowledgments   xv

Introduction   xix

Chronology   xxiii

PART 1: THE LIFE AND WORK OF JOHANN SEBASTIAN BACH

The Bach Family and the Times   3

Early Influences and Childhood   9

Education and Foundations   14

Lüneburg to Weimar   20

Youthful Arrogance   26

Clarification of His Calling   33

Honor and Stability   39

Interlude: Music for Organ   45

Development and Disappointment   49

Deviation from Calling   54

Interlude: Instrumental Music   61

The Early Years in Leipzig: 1720s   64

Interlude: Church Music   73

Conflict and Resolve: 1730s   77

Domestic Life in Leipzig   85

New Heights: 1740s 89

A Dishonored Prophet and Revival 97

PART 2: THE CHARACTER OF JOHANN SEBASTIAN BACH

Accessible Yet Profound 107

Perpetual Learner 111

Faith 115

Humility 119

Just: Pure and Strict Truth 123

Law and Grace 127

Long-suffering 131

Perseverance for What Is Right 135

Preparedness for Death 139

Religious Instructor 144

Respect for the Office of Authority 149

Kindness: Defender of the Weak 153

Freedom Through Limitations 157

Craftsmanship 160

Knowledge 164

Order and Wisdom 168

Teacher 172

Perfection and Excellence 176

Summa: Realized Potential 180

Witness: The St. Matthew Passion 184

Domestic Happiness 188

Family   192

Fun   196

Hospitality   200

Apologia: Mentor for Right Worship   204

Industry   208

Innovative   212

Legacy   216

Patience (Revival)   220

Soli Deo Gloria   224

PART 3: THE LEGACY OF JOHANN SEBASTIAN BACH

Last Church Composer   231

Lasting Legacy   235

The Lessons of Leadership   239

Notes   241

Selected Bibliography   254

Index   257

Foreword

*T*HOUGH KNOWN THROUGHOUT GERMANY and parts of Europe as an accomplished organist and keyboard instructor, Johann Sebastian Bach was not recognized in his own day as a great composer. When he died in 1750, he was buried in an unmarked grave and much of his work was forgotten or lost.

God, however, always honors the name of his servants. And in 1819 Felix Mendelssohn, at the precocious age of ten, received a rare copy of Bach's great oratorio, *St. Matthew's Passion.* He was awestruck. Within eight years Mendelssohn was an accomplished composer and conductor, and he determined to stage a performance of the *Passion.* In 1829 he premiered the *Passion* in Berlin to a packed audience that included Prussian royalty, the philosopher G. W. Hegel, the poet Heinrich Heine, and other notables. Berlin was taken by storm. So great was the demand that the performance was repeated on March 21, Bach's birthday. Germany had rediscovered Bach.

Bach is now recognized as one of the world's greatest (if not the greatest) composers. When Johann Wolfgang von Goethe heard a recital of Bach's organ works, he said, "It is as though eternal harmony were conversing with itself, as it may have happened in God's bosom shortly before He created the world." Richard Wagner referred to Bach's music as "the most stupendous miracle in all music." Robert Schumann claimed that music owes to Bach "almost as great a debt as a religion owes to its founder." And Helmut Walcha, the blind German organist, asserted, "Ultimately, Bach opens a vista to the universe. After experiencing him, people feel there is meaning to life after all."

How would Bach respond to such accolades if he heard them today? He once said: *"Ich habe fleissig sein mussen: wer es gleichfalls ist, wird eben so weit kommen"* (I had to be diligent. Anyone who works as hard will get just as far). Indeed, when asked about his organ playing, Bach humbly replied, "You have only to hit the right notes at the right time, and the instrument plays itself."

Such humility was not a facade. It was a product of Bach's firmly held religious beliefs. It has been said that if there had been no Martin Luther, there would have been no Bach. True indeed. For Bach's entire musical career was a life of religious devotion in the community of the Lutheran Church. He was weaned on Luther's Catechism, read Luther's German Bible, and composed music for Luther's chorales. Bach would not have achieved greatness without his Christian faith.

That modern historians are able to "overlook" the centrality of Bach's faith is a testament to the power of ideology. As you read Gregory Wilbur's insightful treatment of Bach, you will learn many lessons about life and leadership—too many to mention here. But there is another lesson, a broader lesson, to learn here: the significance of faith and world view. Bach is inexplicable apart from his faith. So why do moderns miss this? Because of *their* faith. In other words, world view matters. In fact, it matters so much that it can blind men to the obvious.

As you will see, the author displays both a musician's sensibility and a historian's accuracy. Cutting against the grain of modern historiography, which attempts to ignore or belittle Bach's faith, Wilbur paints a portrait of Bach that is both sympathetic and realistic. No whitewash job here. Just the simple facts. And the most profound facts of Bach's life and work were his mystical devotion to Christ and his desire to labor to the glory of God.

May Wilbur's book create in you a similar devotion and desire.

David J. Vaughan

ACKNOWLEDGMENTS

I AM GREATLY APPRECIATIVE to Ron Pitkin and the folks at Cumberland House for the opportunity to write this book. This work has had a long gestation, and I am pleased to finally be able to bring it to fruition.

To George Grant, the founder and original editor of this series, I thank you for the shared journey of the past decade and the opportunity to learn, grow, and develop under your tutelage as well as to humbly instruct.

I greatly enjoy pithy and witty acknowledgments that make you feel either that you know the people being mentioned or that you wish you knew them. I freely admit that I am incapable of conveying these important people in my life in such a way that you would rush out to meet them; however, I stand firmly in the ideas of the Southern Agrarians and George MacDonald in his wonderful novel *Annals of a Quiet Neighborhood* that the everyday and the ordinary are really the spectacular and the extraordinary. With this in mind, I introduce you to my community.

I am blessed with good friends and wonderful opportunities that help shape my passions and direct my thoughts. Thank you Christ Community Choir, art history and aesthetics classes at Franklin Classical School, Artios Academy, and my own tutorial for the opportunity to put some of these thoughts into practice.

I am thankful particularly for the prayers of my parents, Bob and Barbara Wilbur, and my grandmother, Nana. Thank you Robbie and Chris and Eric for your support and interest. Thank you Lee and Sophia Owen for so completely accepting me into your family. Special thanks also to Patrick and Margaret Showalter (I appreciate your friendship), Gene and Damaris King (for the fun of living in community), Wes King (for your steadfastness and great friendship), Randy, Susan, and Blair Sadler and Mark, Sharon, and Nathan Haney (for sharing your lives and caring for us), Brent and Noele Sadler (for sharing life from afar), and Dean Moyer and William Ashbless (just because).

God has given me an incredible helpmeet in my wife, Sophia. I thank you for your selfless love and sacrifice—as if thanks were sufficient. From the typing of notes to the care of Eleanor, your support and encouragement continue to make me strive, in God's grace, to be a better person. I am so thankful for my family and the home you make for Eleanor and me. (Thank you also for your continued patience in hearing the same Bach music as Eleanor's nightly companion.)

The support of various musical artists graced the writing of this manuscript including: J. S. Bach (not too much of a stretch there!), La Nef, William Byrd, David Diamond, and Thomas Tallis. The list would have been longer except for the extraordinary number of Bach's works that accompanied the writing including the violin concertos (Nigel Kennedy is amazing), the concertos for harpsichord, *Art of Fugue,* oboe concertos, *St. Matthew Passion, St. John Passion, B-minor Mass,* and various sacred cantatas. The more I listen, the more I grow and learn. Sebastian, I thank you for your life and example, and I look forward to meeting you some day.

Pentecost 2005

INTRODUCTION

De artifice non nisi artifex judicare potest—*None but the artist can judge the artist.*[1]

JOHANN SEBASTIAN BACH WAS a musical genius, an intellectual giant, and a gracious man. Art music is often described by the three B's (Bach, Beethoven, and Brahms). Do not forget to add Mozart, Haydn, Wagner, Strauss, Verdi, or Vaughan Williams. For fun, and to sound learned, throw in Tallis, Palestrina, Byrd, Leonin, and Perotin. However, in the final analysis there is really only Bach and everybody else.

Bach's achievement in the area of music is one of the greatest tours de force in the history of the world—on par with, or surpassing, that of Shakespeare, Michelangelo, Dante, Leonardo, Rembrandt, Milton, Aristotle, Augustine, or Aquinas. Bach was that great and that significant. Even more compelling is the fact that he consciously and deliberately wrote all of his music from a Christian perspective and for the glory of God.

To adequately be able to access and understand Bach would require someone of the same stature as Bach. For the rest of us, all we can do is scratch at the surface and be astonished at accomplishments that astound and amaze. The depths of his music are so profound that experts could spend a lifetime delving into the wonders of a single work—yet there are nearly a thousand works extant. The task is monumental. Bach's handwritten musical manuscripts total tens of thousands of pages. I must agree with biographer Johann Nikolaus Forkel, who wrote in 1802, "I am, on the contrary, thoroughly convinced that no language in the world is rich enough to express all that might and should be said of the astonishing extent of such a genius. The more intimately we are acquainted with it, the more does our admiration increase. All our eulogiums, praises, and admiration will always be and remain no more than well-meant prattle."[2]

This work seeks to present the leadership traits of this godly and creative man in an introductory manner. Such a task is impossible without reference to his actual work. I have kept the musical discussion on a layman's level with the goal of trying to convey somewhat the accomplishments of Bach as a composer that relate directly to an understanding of his leadership. To that end, the "Interlude" chapters relate specific information about Bach's compositions that correspond to the period discussed in his life in the preceding chapter. I found this method less cumbersome to the narrative flow of the biography than to include all of the musical information chronologically. There are, of course, many resources to aid in the pursuit of greater knowledge with regard to any of these works.

The period of the Baroque stretched from around 1600 to the year 1750, which deliberately coincides with the

death of Bach. In music, the Baroque period was a corrective to the Renaissance tendency to present ethereal
music that was lofty and airy. Melody lines appeared in all
voice parts simultaneously, with a subservient instrumental role. As such, Renaissance music eventually tended to
distance itself from the people. The Baroque influence
consisted of the representation of emotion and a clear
structure. Musically this translated to a melody rooted by
a foundation of harmony. Renaissance music tends to be
horizontal in its approach; Baroque music is more vertical.
The genius of Bach is that his music functions both horizontally as well as vertically.

Bach was able to function on a multiplicity of levels: a
conservator of past styles and musical elements and an in-
novator of new forms and styles; a craftsman who brought
his art to the highest imaginable summit while creating
timeless works of beauty; an artisan who perfected his art
with almost scientific precision while remaining lively and
accessible to average listeners; a communicator who
clearly conveyed a message while simultaneously embed-
ding layers of symbolism—musical and extramusical—
that require studious inquiry to uncover.

Bach worked at a crucial time in the history of the
church, combating the ideas of the Enlightenment and
the elevation of human reason. Bach's struggles, musically
and professionally, are those of a man seeking to maintain
a high view of worship, academics, and a view of all of life
grounded on the Word of God. Bach sought to preserve
and elevate the worship of the church against specific foes
who attempted to undermine his very work. As a man
valiant in his convictions, he stood against the trends and

fashions of his day and succeeded as a witness of the gospel to subsequent generations.

I have come to love this man passionately. I mourn his loss and, even greater, the lack of subsequent Bachs to champion the place of good theology and excellent art, to stand *contra mundum* to the prevailing secular ideologies, and to comprehend the arts from a truly biblical manner for the purpose of edifying and instructing the church and for the glory of Almighty God. It is my prayer that this small volume might be a step in that direction.

CHRONOLOGY

1685	Johann Sebastian Bach was born on March 21 in Eisenach, Thuringia, where his father was a musician.
1693	Enrolled in the Latin School in Eisenach.
1694	His mother, Elisabetha, died in May.
1695	His father, Ambrosius, died in February. Bach moved to Ohrdruf and lived with his brother, Johann Christoph.
1700	He left home to study at St. Michael's School in Lüneburg. He walked the two hundred miles to get to the school.
1701	Anna Magdalena Wülken was born on September 22, the daughter of a court trumpeter in Zeitz.
1702	His formal education ended as he had no money to continue his education at a university—a fact that would continue to plague him throughout his career.
1703	He served as a violinist in the chamber orchestra of Johann Ernst, the younger brother of the Duke of Weimar. He was treated as a servant.
	In the summer, Bach was invited to try out the newly renovated organ at the church in Arnstadt. Despite the fact that the church already had an organist, he was offered a position on August 9.
	Bach moved to Arnstadt.
1705	Maria Barbara, an orphan, came to live with her aunt and uncle at the Golden Crown Inn where Sebastian also lived.

He had a physical altercation with Geysersbach, a bassoonist he had insulted.

He asked for a month's leave to travel 250 miles on foot to Lübeck in order to hear the Advent vesper services of organist and composer Dietrich Buxtehude.

1706   After a stay of four months, Bach was offered Buxtehude's position upon his retirement with the stipulation that he marry Buxtehude's spinster daughter.

He returned to Arnstadt in February with more clearly defined ideas and conviction about the role of music in aiding worship.

1707   Bach left Arnstadt and filled a civic position in the free imperial city of Mühlhausen.

October 17: He married Barbara in Dornheim.

1708   He composed an elaborate cantata for the church service in February to celebrate and install new city council members. The council ordered the work to be printed in the city records—the only church cantata printed during Bach's life.

He left his employment in Mühlhausen on June 25 for a position with Duke Wilhelm Ernst, who included an additional allowance of coal so that Bach could practice in the heated chapel during winter.

His first daughter, Catharina Dorothea Bach, was born in December.

1710   Wilhelm Friedemann was born on November 22.

1713   Barbara gave birth to twins on February 23, but they both died within the first month.

1714   Bach was promoted to concert master in Weimar on March 2.

Carl Philipp Emanuel was born on March 8. Composer Georg Philipp Telemann was his godfather.

Bach's first Weimar cantata was performed on March 25—Palm Sunday.

1715 Johann Gottfried Bernhard was born on May 11.

1716 He was passed over for a promotion to the rank of capellmeister and began to look for another position.

1717 His visit to Dresden included a contest with Marchand, who fled after he heard Sebastian play.

He accepted a position with Prince Leopold of Saxe-Cöthen. Bach was hauled off to jail because Duke Wilhelm Ernst refused to release him.

He was granted an unfavorable discharge in December after spending a month in jail.

He moved to Cöthen, where Prince Leopold was a sympathetic and gifted musician and friend.

1718 Barbara bore a son on November 17 who died soon afterward.

1719 Internationally famous composer G. F. Handel visited his mother in nearby Halle. Bach tried to make contact with him but failed.

1720 He traveled with the prince to Carlsbad in May. When he returned, he discovered that Barbara had died and had already been buried.

1721 The six *Brandenburg Concertos* were completed by March 24 and dedicated to Christian Ludwig, margrave of Brandenburg.

He met Anna Magdalena, a court singer, in September.

He married Anna Magdalena in December. He was thirty-six and she was twenty.

Prince Leopold married a woman who had no interest in

music and who was jealous of her husband's activities (especially his friendship with Bach).

1722 He completed the twenty-four preludes and fugues of *The Well-Tempered Clavier.*

In December, Bach became a candidate for the position of cantor in Leipzig.

1723 Bach accepted a lower position as municipal cantor in Leipzig on May 5.

Christiana Sophia Henrietta, the first child of Anna Magdalena, was born.

May 22: Bach and his family arrived in Leipzig.

May 30: Bach held his first cantata performance in Leipzig.

1724 Gottfried Heinrich was born on February 27.

The *St. John Passion* was first performed on Good Friday, April 7.

June 11 marked the start of Bach's second cycle of church cantatas in Leipzig.

1725 Christian Gottlieb was born and later baptized on April 14.

Bach gave an organ recital in Dresden in September.

1726 Elizabet Juliana Friederica was baptized on April 5. Christiana Sophia Henrietta died on June 29 at the age of three.

1727 The *St. Matthew Passion* was first performed on Good Friday, April 11.

Ernestus Andreas was baptized on October 30 and died on November 1.

1728 Son Christian Gottlieb died on September 21 at the age of three.

Regina Johanna was baptized on October 10.

1729 Bach traveled to Cöthen in March to present the funeral cantata for Prince Leopold.

Bach assumed the directorship of the *Collegium Musicum* at Zimmermann's Coffeehouse.

In June, G. F. Handel was once again in Halle, but an invitation to visit Bach in Leipzig met with failure.

1730   Christiana Benedicta was baptized on January 1 and died on January 4.

1731   Christiana Dorothea was baptized on March 18.

Bach gave an organ recital in Dresden and other performances at court.

1732   Johann Christoph Friedrich was born on June 21.

Christiana Dorothea died on August 31 at the age of one.

1733   Regina Johanna died on April 25 at the age of four.

Oldest son Wilhelm Friedemann was appointed organist at St. Sophia's Church in Dresden.

In July, Bach presented his *Kyrie* and *Gloria* to Friedrich August II with a request for a court title.

Johann August Abraham was baptized on November 5 and died November 6.

1734   Rector Johann August Ernesti became Sebastian's superior, but he had little regard and tolerance for church music or Sebastian.

1734–35   The *Christmas Oratorio* was first performed in six parts on the feast days from Christmas to Epiphany.

1735   He composed the "Coffee" cantata.

Johann Christian was born on September 5.

1736   Bach received the title of court composer to the elector of Saxony.

1737   Johanna Carolina was baptized on October 30.

1738   Son Carl Philipp Emanuel was appointed harpsichordist for Frederick the Great of Prussia.

1739	Johann Gottfried Bernhard died on May 27.
1741	*Clavier-Übung IV,* the "Goldberg Variations," published.
1742	His last child, Regina Susanna, was baptized on February 22.
1747	Bach visited Potsdam and performed for Frederick II of Prussia in May.
1747	In June, Bach joined Mizler's Corresponding Society of the Musical Science.
1749	On January 20 Bach's daughter Elisabeth Juliana Friederica married Bach's pupil Johann Christoph Altnickol.
	The municipal committee heard an audition for a replacement for Bach in June.
1750	In March, Bach underwent eye surgery twice.
	Bach died on July 28. He was buried on July 31 with no eulogy or grave marker.
1751	The *Art of Fugue* was published in May.
1754	Mizler published Bach's obituary as written by Carl Philipp Emanuel and Johann Friedrich Agricola.
1760	In February, Anna Magdalena died in an almshouse and was given a pauper's funeral and burial.
1802	Johann Nikolaus Forkel published his biography of Bach.
1829	Felix Mendelssohn conducted the *St. Matthew Passion* to great acclaim.
1840	Prince Albert introduced Bach's music in concerts at Buckingham Palace and Windsor Castle after his marriage to Queen Victoria.
1850	The *Bach-Gesellschaft,* established in part by Franz Liszt and Robert Schumann, started the process of publishing the complete works of Bach—a task that took fifty years to complete.

Part 1

The Life and Work of Johann Sebastian Bach

The aim and final end of all music should be none other than the glory of God and the refreshment of the soul.

—Johann Sebastian Bach

The Bach Family and the Times

*More than anyone else, J.S. Bach symbolizes
music that grows out of, yet moves beyond
worship . . . Bach is the musical result of Luther.[1]*

O n March 21, 1685, the eighth and last child
of Ambrosius and Elisabeth Bach was born in
Eisenach, Thuringia. Johann Sebastian was christened two
days later at the baptismal font in the historic St. George's
Church (*Georgenkirche*) in Eisenach, with one of Ambrosius's colleagues acting as godfather and supplying the
name "Sebastian."[2] Sebastian was the heir and culmination
of a long line of family musicians, recognized for their talent and known for their fierce family bonds and strong adherence to the Reformation teaching of Martin Luther.

In 1735 Sebastian Bach memorialized the history of his
family in a set a genealogical notes he entitled "Origin of
the Musical Bach Family." His son Carl Philipp Emanuel
Bach continued to make additions to the document after
the death of his father. In this record, Bach recounted the
history of Veit Bach, the patriarch of the Bach clan. Veit

was a native of Ungarn, a region that comprised parts of Moravia, Slovakia, and Hungary.[3] A "white-bread baker" by trade, he took his son, Johannes, and fled his homeland in the late sixteenth century to escape religious persecution "on account of his Lutheran religion."[4] As Bach wrote, "After [he] converted his property into money, so far as might be, he moved to Germany; and, finding adequate security for the Lutheran religion in Thuringia, settled at Wechmar, near Gotha, and continued in his baker's trade there."[5]

Bach made mention of his forebear's penchant for music making as well. "[Veit] found his greatest pleasure in a little cittern, which he took with him even into the mill and played upon while the grinding was going on. (How pretty it must have sounded together! Yet in this way he had a chance to have time drilled into him.) And this was, as it were, the beginning of a musical inclination in his descendants."[6] A cittern is a small ten-stringed instrument much like a modern mandolin. Veit died in March 1619.

Veit's son, Johannes, started his professional life as a baker like his father but became a professional musician after apprenticing to the town piper at Gotha. He lived in Wechmar but traveled to various towns to assist in music making, including Gotha, Arnstadt, Erfurt, and Eisenach—all towns that continued to be associated with Bach family musicians. Over the next seven generations, this humble Wechmar line of Bachs "produced over seventy sons who earned their living as musicians"[7]—an astonishing legacy by any standard.

Thuringia is a province in central Germany. After the Thirty Years' War ended in 1648, Thuringia made a quick recovery. Its location at the center of important trade routes that ran east and west as well as north and south made Thuringia a dynamic region with regard to both economics and culture. As a crossroads district, many different influences passed through this region.[8] "Thuringia was one of the most musical districts in Germany in the seventeenth century, and was also a stronghold of the reformed religion. From this and its neighboring districts the Bachs never wandered."[9]

One of Thuringia's favorite sons was Martin Luther (1483–1546), leader of the German Reformation. In addition to his theological reforms, Luther also reformed the practice of music in worship. Luther believed music to be a gift from God *(donum Dei)* instead of a human invention. As such, he intertwined concepts of music and theology.[10] Luther wrote about music in the following words:

> I would certainly like to praise music with all my heart as the excellent gift of God which it is and to commend it to everyone . . . next to the Word of God, music deserves the highest praise.

> I plainly judge, and do not hesitate to affirm, that except for theology there is no art that could be put on the same level with music. . . .

> God has cheered our heart and minds through his dear Son, whom he gave to redeem us from sin, death, and the devil. He who believes this earnestly cannot be quiet about it. But he must gladly and willingly sing and speak about it so others also may come to hear it. And whoever

does not want to sing and speak of it shows that he does
not believe and that he does not belong under the new
joyful testament.[11]

Luther incorporated music into the life of the church
through the introduction of vernacular chorales or
hymns. Rich with doctrine, this body of chorales was
commonly known by the people and enthusiastically
sung weekly. Eventually, each Sunday and feast day in
the church calendar had specific hymns associated with
it, which provided a musical correlation between the
preaching of the Word, the lives of the congregants, and
the music they sang.

Luther went to the Latin School in Eisenach that Sebastian Bach attended two hundred years later. In 1521,
Luther took refuge in Eisenach at the Wartburg Castle, a
medieval hilltop castle that overlooks the town. It was
there that he translated the Greek New Testament into
German. Wartburg was also the site of a famous Tourney
of Song in 1207, which matched the best German min-
strels against one another in competition.[12]

The church in Eisenach, St. George's, dated back to
1182. Rebuilt in 1515, Luther preached there twice in
the spring of 1521 on his way to and returning from the
Diet of Worms.[13] The three galleries in the nave of the
church gave it a capacity of more than two thousand
worshipers.[14] The Bach family would have had difficulty
finding another region so closely aligned to their own
beliefs.

Johann Ambrosius Bach, Sebastian's father, was born in
Erfurt in 1645 and married Elisabeth Lämmerhirt, the

daughter of a town councillor in Erfurt.[15] At this time, there were essentially three ways that a German musician could earn a living in his chosen profession. The first was in the "service of a noble or princely patron as court or chamber musician," the second was in the service "of a town council as town piper," and the third was in the service "of a municipal or ecclesiastical authority as church organist, music director, or cantor—the latter function including the teaching of music in a school."[16] Ambrosius was the second of these—a *Hausmann,* or town piper. In October 1671 Ambrosius moved to Eisenach to take up his new duties.

Ambrosius was responsible for playing trumpet twice daily from the tower of the town hall overlooking the market square. These performances of dances or chorale tunes took place at 10:00 a.m. and 5:00 p.m. with a band of half a dozen players. In addition, Ambrosius played violin at St. George's Church each Sunday and on feast days. Extra duties included playing at civic functions, weddings, funerals, and private occasions. In the 1670s he also became a member of the court orchestra.[17]

Highly regarded by his fellow townsmen, the city council refused to release him from his job in 1684 to accept another post. As biographer Christoph Wolff explained:

References to his extraordinary kind of music making appear early on. One document, which exempts him from the local brewery tax, not only points to his Christian virtues and moral conduct but praises "his particular professional qualifications, in that he can come up with vocal and instrumental music for worship service and for honorable assemblies with persons of higher and lower ranks in such a way that we cannot remember having ever experienced anything like it in this place." Similarly, a town chronicler's report displays unparalleled enthusiasm: "In 1672 at Easter the new town piper made music with organ, violins, voices, trumpets and military drums, as had never before been done by any cantor or town musician as long as Eisenach stood."[18]

Not only did Sebastian Bach enter into a family with a gifted and talented father, the Bach clan was so musically inclined that the name Bach became synonymous with "musician." As such, there were "musical Bachs in Arnstadt and Eisenach, in Ohrdruf, Hamburg, and Lüneburg, in Berlin, Schweinfurt, and Halle, in Dresden, Gotha, Weimar, Jena, Mühlhausen, Minden, and Leipzig."[19] However, no one combined the depths of theological understanding with the heights of artistic expression that Johann Sebastian achieved throughout his life. A product of a prodigious and productive family, he developed into the summit of artistic achievement.

EARLY INFLUENCES AND CHILDHOOD

*The best method of instructing youth, therefore, is
to accustom them to what is good. The right
understanding of it follows in time, and can then
still further confirm their attachment to none but
genuine works of art.*[20]

*J*OHANN WAS A FAVORITE family name of the Bachs.
In fact, all of Ambrosius's six sons and his twin
brother's four sons were named Johann. At the time Ambrosius and his wife moved to Eisenach in 1671, they
brought with them a four-month-old son, Johann Christoph. Their oldest child had previously died before the age
of six months. In Eisenach, they had six more children: Johann Balthasar, Johannes Jonas, Maria Salome, Johanna
Juditha, Johann Jacob, and Johann Sebastian. Jonas died
in 1685 at the age of ten (Sebastian was two months old),
and Juditha died in 1686 at the age of six. Also in 1686,
Christoph left home at the age of fifteen to study music
with Johann Pachelbel in Erfurt. When Sebastian was six
years old, his brother Balthasar, who had served as an apprentice to their father for three years, died at the age of

eighteen. Therefore, Sebastian lived with only two siblings from the age of six on.[21]

However, the Bach home was anything but empty or quiet. As part of the Bach legacy of caring for others, homes were always open for relatives in need. In his home over various periods of time, Ambrosius provided for his younger sister, who was severely physically and mentally handicapped (until her death); his wife's widowed mother (until her death); the son of a cousin who died in the plague; and the orphaned son of another cousin (for eleven years).[22] In addition, as town piper Ambrosius also trained several apprentices at a time. Normally an extra three people between the ages of fifteen and twenty lived with the Bachs while they learned their trade from Ambrosius.[23]

Sebastian's home was the center of professional music in the town of Eisenach. As such, from an early age he "absorbed an atmosphere dominated by music" that involved the entire family and those who lived with them.[24] The musical activities at the house were "not merely teaching, practicing, rehearsing, and performing, but also . . . collecting and copying music, repairing and maintaining musical instruments, and other endeavors related to an extended music-business establishment."[25] The position of town piper indicated a proficiency in a number of instruments. Most likely, Ambrosius played and taught students on violin, oboe, transverse flute, trumpet and horn, and the remaining brass instruments.

In Eisenach, the four foundations of seventeenth-century German musical culture were situated within a one-eighth-mile diameter: church, town, school, and

court. The town hall represented the location for official
and public music events; the dual castle had its court
capelle, or orchestra, of which Ambrosius was a member;
the St. George Latin School included the *chorus musicus*
(student choir) as an integrated part of its curriculum; and
St. George's Church with organ and choir loft was the
home of sacred music.[26] Bach's family actively participated in all of these venues of musical activity.

The organist at St. George's Church, Johann Christoph
Bach, was a cousin of Ambrosius. Sebastian called him "a
profound composer" in his genealogy.[27] Records indicate
that the organ at St. George's Church was in need of constant attention and repair during the 1690s. Presumably,
young Sebastian had the opportunity at an early age to
crawl among the inner workings of his cousin's organ and
learn from the inside out.[28]

Scripture, Luther's catechism, music, and Latin formed
the basis of the curriculum at the Latin School in Eisenach. Arithmetic, history, Greek, Hebrew, philosophy,
logic, and rhetoric completed the rest of the studies on
various levels.[29] The school was divided into six sections
based on achievement and not necessarily age: the *sexta*
was the beginning or lowest level, with the *prima* as the
final level. Students normally spent about two years per
level.[30] Sebastian entered the school at the *quinta* level, indicating that at the age of eight he had already mastered
the material in the *sexta* and could read and write. Instruction from the fourth class onward utilized Latin as
the primary language of instruction.[31]

The school day consisted of two half-day teaching periods, with the first session lasting from 6:00 to 9:00 a.m. in

summer (7:00–10:00 a.m. in winter) on Monday through Saturday. The second session lasted from 1:00 to 3:00 p.m., with no classes on Wednesday or Saturday afternoons. The *chorus musicus* rehearsed four days a week from 12:00 to 1:00 p.m.[32] Records indicate that Sebastian was a superior student at the Latin School.[33]

Sebastian also sang in the choir at St. George's Church. With his father playing violin and his cousin at the organ, one wonders how many other Bachs and family friends made up the musical complement from week to week.[34]

On May 3, 1694, Sebastian's mother died. Ambrosius had lost his twin brother the previous year, and now, after twenty-six years of marriage, he was a widower.[35] With three children remaining at home (not to mention apprentices and relatives), Ambrosius sought a suitable stepmother to care for the household. In true Bach fashion, he proposed to and was accepted by Barbara Margaretha, the widow of first cousin Johann Günther Bach of Arnstadt. At the age of thirty-five, Margaretha was twice a widow with two daughters, ages ten and twelve, under her care. Ambrosius was able to provide for his own children and the family of a kinsman in one stroke. The two were married in Eisenach on November 27, 1694.[36]

"Twelve weeks and one day" into their marriage, as Margaretha put it, Ambrosius died, leaving Bach an orphan and Margaretha a widow yet again. Just before his tenth birthday in 1695, Sebastian was deprived of both mother and father, as well as the rich musical life of which he had been a part. Margaretha apparently sold the house in Eisenach and moved with her daughters back to Arnstadt, where nothing more is known of them. Sebastian's older sister, Maria Salome, joined her mother's relatives in Erfurt; and Jacob and Sebastian moved to their brother Christoph's home in Ohrdruf.[37]

In the first ten years of life, Sebastian benefited from a classical Christian education steeped in Reformation theology and numerous and varied musical activities and experiences. These opportunities formed the foundation of his great achievements. In speaking of the education of his own sons, Bach said, "Because they had, from their earliest youth, opportunity in their father's house to hear good music, and no other. They were therefore accustomed early, and even before they had received any instruction, to what was most excellent in the art."[38] No doubt the same could be said for Bach's own upbringing.

In addition, Bach lived with loss from a very early age. The presence of the subject of death that pervades his later vocal work no doubt stemmed from the deaths of loved ones in his early years (as well as other subsequent losses). However, the sense of hope in eternal life because of Christ the Redeemer provides an answer and solace to this loss. This understanding, too, is a product of his theology lessons as a young child.

EDUCATION AND FOUNDATIONS

*Now there is music from which a man can
learn something.*

—W. A. MOZART (1756–91)[39]

*B*ACH SCHOLAR CHRISTOPH WOLFF summed up
Bach's childhood experiences like this:

Without a doubt Sebastian was brought up from his earliest childhood days to observe the virtues of perseverance
and constant hard work. Extreme industriousness is,
however, but one side. The musical experiences that
shaped Sebastian through his formative years are almost
unparalleled in their quality, variety, and extent. Besides
being born into a family of musicians that included great-
grandfather, grandfather, father, three brothers, and numerous uncles and cousins, and being in the constant
company of journeymen, apprentices, and colleagues
around his parents' and uncles' houses, the thoroughly
professional surroundings in which he grew up exposed
him to all major facets of musical culture: instrumental

and vocal, ensemble and solo, sacred, and secular, performed at home or in town, court, or school. Sebastian had to understand this multifaceted setting as unified—from the more workmanlike making and maintenance of instruments, preparation of performing materials, and commissioning and contracting of deals all the way up to the artistic aspects of performance and the creation of new music.[40]

Such continued to be the case as Sebastian and Jacob settled into their new lives with their older brother Christoph in Ohrdruf. Christoph left his parents' home in Eisenach when he was fifteen years old to study with Johann Pachelbel in Erfurt. Sebastian was one year old when Christoph left.

Christoph studied for three years with Pachelbel. During his third year he also held the post of organist at St. Thomas's Church in Erfurt. He then moved to Arnstadt to assist his ailing uncle Heinrich in the completion of his various organ duties at three of the churches in that town. After a year there, Christoph accepted the post of organist at St. Michael's Church in Ohrdruf. He was eighteen at the time.[41] These varied experiences speak to his ability and responsibility from an early age.

Orhdruf was a small town of about twenty-five hundred people situated at the foot of the Thuringian Forest and about twenty-five miles south of Eisenach. In 727, St. Boniface and a group of Scottish-Irish missionary monks established a small monastery with St. Michael's chapel. This location provided the site for a larger church built in the early 1400s.[42]

Christoph married Johanna Dorothea Vonhoff in October 1694, and they were expecting their firstborn child at the time that Jacob and Sebastian came to live with them in March 1695. Their son Tobias Friedrich was born in July 1695. They ultimately had six sons and three daughters. Two of their sons eventually studied music with Sebastian when he lived in Weimar and Leipzig. Their youngest son was named Johann Sebastian, but he died as a child.[43] Jacob stayed with his brother and sister-in-law until the following year, when he returned to Eisenach as an apprentice to the town piper who succeeded his father, Ambrosius.[44]

Christoph struggled with the financial burden of an unexpectedly growing family, but Sebastian was able to receive financial assistance to attend the Latin School in Orhdruf. The school utilized Latin grammar and theology as the basis of the curriculum. In addition, geography, history, arithmetic, and natural science, along with logic and rhetoric, formed the core classes. Music played a prominent role in the education, with four hours a week devoted to music study in the third and fourth classes, and five hours a week in the first and second classes.[45]

In 1697, Bach graduated from the *tertia,* the third class, as both the youngest and the top student. At the age of fourteen, he achieved promotion to the *prima,* or first class, a full two years younger than the average student. All of his other brothers had left school at the age of fourteen or fifteen when they completed the third class.[46] Bach maintained his early promise as an excellent scholar.

Christoph taught Sebastian how to play the clavier (a general name for keyboard stringed instruments such as harpsichord, clavichord, etc.). Apparently Christoph did not teach Sebastian as quickly as he desired, and he asked his older brother for access to a book of copied music that Christoph kept locked in a cupboard. He denied his younger brother this opportunity because of the complexity of the music and the value of the book. However, since the doors to the cupboard consisted of latticework, Sebastian was able to pass his small hands through the openings, roll up the manuscript, and extract it through the modest holes. This he did at night when circumstances favored it. "But, for want of a candle, he could only copy it in the moonlight nights; and it took six whole months before he could finish his laborious task."[47] Apparently Sebastian tried to practice the new pieces in secret. But when Christoph discovered Sebastian's deed, he took the newly created manuscript away from him. Sebastian did not recover his book until the death of his brother, twenty years later.[48] Such was Sebastian's insatiable appetite to learn new things, to overcome obstacles, and to be challenged beyond his years.

By the time he was fifteen years old, Bach had already studied five areas of music through the instruction of his father, brother, and school. His training included vocal (for which he had an "uncommonly fine soprano voice"),[49] violin, keyboard instruction in both harpsichord and organ (under Christoph's guidance), and composition.[50] In addition, Bach presumably gained more experience in the machinery and maintenance of organs. Christoph's organs at St. Michael's Church required nearly constant attention to keep them in a playable condition—a task highly suitable for the assistance of a young teenager.[51] His vocal studies and singing opportunities exposed him to solos, liturgical plainsong (chant), and polyphonic music. Of course the musical staple was the German chorale. Sebastian grew up with the Eisenach hymnal of 1673—with more than a thousand pages and six hundred hymns, Bach was well-versed in the songs of the Reformation.[52]

At that time, the primary method of learning and teaching particular subjects was through imitation. Students learning writing or music skills memorized and copied the *exempla classica,* or exemplary classics, of eminent and distinguished masters.[53] Emulation of the classics provided a firm foundation in what was excellent and a model on which to base new creative work. This concept also reflected the medieval and Baroque concept that craftsmanship was of greater importance than originality—a view contradicting that held by the emerging secular Enlightenment, which placed individuality and originality above all else.

By early 1700 a lack of financial assistance caused Bach to make some decisions regarding his education. At his age, all of his brothers had left school and pursued a career in music; however, Bach still wanted the opportunity to continue his schooling. Bach's choral instructor for most of his time in Orhdruf was a man named Elias Herder. From 1689 to 1695, Herder had been a choral scholar at St. Michael's School in Lüneburg, some two hundred miles to the north. With Herder's encouragement and contacts, Bach secured a financial-need scholarship to continue his education. Leaving with him for the same reasons was his slightly older friend Georg Erdmann.[54] Some twenty-five years later, Bach fondly referred to Erdmann as an "erstwhile schoolmate and travel companion."[55]

In mid-March 1700 Bach and Erdmann set out on foot for the two-hundred-mile trek north to Lüneburg.[56] Bach was leaving the province of Thuringia and the sphere of Bach family influence for the first time.

LÜNEBURG TO WEIMAR

Playing and studying Bach convinces us that we are all numbskulls.

—ROBERT SCHUMANN (1810–56)[57]

$\mathcal{W}$ITH A POPULATION OF around ten thousand, Lüneburg was by far the largest city in which Bach had lived. For Bach, Lüneburg possessed the added attraction of being in close proximity to Hamburg, the largest city in Germany with a long and dynamic musical tradition and a reputation for fine organists.[58] Bach and Erdmann arrived at St. Michael's School after their two-hundred-mile sojourn in time to sing as part of the choir on Saturday, April 3, 1700, the day before Palm Sunday. Their first services were vespers on Saturday afternoon, followed by a 6:00 a.m. Sunday matins and 7:15 a.m. main church service the next day.[59] Clearly Bach and Erdmann did not waste any time integrating themselves into the life of the school and the related church services.

Both Bach and Erdmann were admitted into the select singing group known as the "matins scholars." This ensemble consisted of about fifteen members and was responsible for additional performances, and also received greater benefits than other students at St. Michael's. Daily matins services in the mornings, Sunday services, and feast days comprised the bulk of their singing; however, the matins scholars also sang at weddings, funerals, social events, and even through the streets, which provided the choral scholars with additional funds.[60] Bach's music scholarship provided for tuition, room and board, candles and firewood, and a small stipend, with the potential of more money from the incidental performances.[61] When Bach's voice changed (which at that time did not normally occur until around age seventeen), he transferred to playing violin with the accompanying orchestra and acting as rehearsal accompanist for the choir.[62]

The library at St. Michael's School started its collection in 1555. By 1696, the library boasted some eleven hundred manuscript volumes of music by at least 175 different composers—an amazing resource that provided the music scholars with a vast variety of music.[63] In addition to the excellent library, the standards of music instruction and performance were quite high. The school curriculum consisted of Latin and Greek, logic, rhetoric, religion, and music. St. Michael's Church, where the music scholars sang for worship, must have provided further inspiration to Bach with its "colorful church symbols, High Altar, pulpit with spreading canopy, majestic organ façade, and many other appointments."[64]

Adjoining the St. Michael's School was the Ritteracademie—a finishing school for the sons of noblemen that taught French, fencing, and dancing.[65] The interaction among the students in the two schools provided the sons of noblemen with lackeys and the St. Michael students with social polishing and incidental funds. Most likely, Lüneburg was the source of Bach's knowledge of French and Italian.[66]

Bach cultivated a relationship with and probably studied with the great organist Georg Böhm in Lüneburg. This connection led to the opportunity to travel to Hamburg to hear and meet the dean of the great north German organists, Johann Adam Reinken.[67] Johann Nikolaus Forkel, author of an 1802 biography of Bach, described in the following manner Bach's insatiable desire to gain musical experience:

> His inclination to play on the clavier and organ was as ardent at this time as in his more early years and impelled him to try to do, and see, and to hear everything which, according to the ideas he then entertained, could contribute to his improvement. With this view he not only went several times, while he was a scholar, from Lüneburg to Hamburg to hear the organist John Adam Reinken, who was at that time very famous, but sometimes also to Celle in order to get acquainted with the Prince's band, which consisted chiefly of Frenchmen, and with the French taste, which was then a novelty in those parts.[68]

Hamburg was the musical center of north Germany, and Bach walked the thirty miles to the city on numerous occasions in order to hear Reinken play his magnificent organ at St. Catherine's Church. Bach even had the opportunity to play for Reinken, who was almost eighty years old at the time. The octogenarian encouraged the teenager, who must have already possessed a prodigious talent.[69] Reinken had been a student of the great Netherlander organist and composer Jan Pieterszon Sweelinck.[70] Bach's ideas about organ playing and the construction and potential of the organ itself were shaped by his exposure to Reinken and his playing. While in Hamburg, Bach made contacts with other organists and even went to the opera.[71]

Bach's cousin Johann Ernst (1683–1739) lived in Hamburg—previously the two of them had gone to school together in Ohrdruf. The presence of family must have helped to offset the cost of traveling back and forth; however, Bach's trips placed a strain upon his finances. This situation is illustrated by a story that Bach "used to remember with pleasure":

> Since he made several trips to hear this master, it happened one day, since he stayed longer in Hamburg than the state of his purse permitted, that on his way home to Lüneburg he had only a couple of schillings in his pocket. He had not gotten halfway home yet when he developed a keen appetite, and accordingly went into an inn, where the savory odors from the kitchen only made the state in which he found himself ten times more painful. In the midst of his sad meditations on this subject, he heard the grinding noise of a window opening and saw a pair of herring heads thrown out onto the rubbish pile. Since he was a true Thuringian, the sight of these heads made his mouth begin to water and he lost not a second in taking possession of them. And lo and behold! he had hardly started to tear them apart when he found a Danish ducat

hidden in each head. This find enabled him not only to add a portion of roast meat to his meal but also at the first opportunity to make another pilgrimage, in greater comfort, to Mr. Reinecke in Hamburg.[72]

The chance that the anonymous benefactor was a student at the Ritteracademie is a distinct possibility.

Bach's financial situation made it impossible for him to receive composition lessons from a professional musician. No music publishing firms existed in Germany at that time, and print music from Italy or England was expensive.[73] By Easter 1702 Bach had completed his final year in the upper class at St. Michael's School. His decision not to continue with a university degree may have been a financial necessity as well as a choice. He had continued his education further than any of his near relatives.[74] He now had to figure out a way to make a living on his own.

Bach submitted to a probe, or audition, for an organist position at St. Jacob's Church in Sangerhausen. Despite the fact that he was only seventeen and had no experience, the committee offered him the position. However, the Duke of Saxe-Weissenfels intervened in the selection process in order to obtain the job for his own candidate. Thirty-four years later, Bach referred to this incident in a letter to the church in Sangerhausen recommending his son Johann Gottfried Bernhard for the position of organist, which he himself had been denied.[75]

Bach accepted a position as violinist to the court *capelle,* or orchestra, in Weimar in January 1703. His position was that of a lackey and included nonmusical chores and valet services.[76] He wore livery, ate and slept with the servants, and entered and left the palace by the rear door. Bach stayed in Weimar for only six months, but in that time he gained exposure to Italian instrumental music, which became influential in his development as a composer.[77]

In July 1703 representatives from the New Church in Arnstadt invited Bach to examine and try out their new organ. After his playing of the instrument, they immediately offered him a job at a salary more than their current organist's. Bach accepted the position and moved to Arnstadt in August 1703. For a young man of eighteen, the prospect of commanding a new organ in a church position was an amazing opportunity and a testimony to his abilities.

YOUTHFUL ARROGANCE
ARNSTADT: 1703–7

*He should behave in the future quite differently
and better than he had hitherto, or the favor
meant for him would be withdrawn.*

—REBUKE OF BACH FROM THE ARNSTADT
CONSISTORY, FEBRUARY 21, 1706[78]

*N*EW CHURCH IN ARNSTADT was formerly
known as St. Boniface but formally known
as St. Sophia. Fire destroyed the medieval St. Boniface
Church in 1581, along with the municipal offices and
more than four hundred homes in Arnstadt. Since there
were other churches in town, the need to rebuild St.
Boniface was not great, and the rebuilding did not occur
until Sophia, Countess of Schwarzburg, donated money
in 1676—hence the new official name of St. Sophia.
With the completion of the church in 1683, the towns-
people commonly referred to it as the New Church. The
organ was completed in 1703.[79]

Situated on the edge of the mountainous Thuringian
Forest, Arnstadt was the oldest city in Thuringia, with a
city charter granted in 1266 and documentation of its existence dating back to 704.[80] With a population of thirty-

eight hundred people, Arnstadt was the principal town in the province of Schwarzburg-Arnstadt. The Bach family had had a presence in the town since around 1620. The town employed Caspar Bach (who died before 1644) and four of his sons as musicians. Ambrosius and Johann Christoph Bach, Sebastian's father and uncle, both worked in Arnstadt—Ambrosius from 1654 to 1667, and Christoph from 1671 to 1693 as a court musician. Heinrich Bach, whom Sebastian's brother Christoph aided in the late 1680s, served as organist at the two principal churches for more than fifty years until his death in 1692. Bach's family reputation and the presence of family connections still living in Arnstadt probably helped recommend him for the opportunity to examine and try out the new organ at the New Church. At age eighteen, Bach's professional qualifications were slight for such a task; however, he had grown up in Eisenach around his cousin's organ, which frequently needed repair; his brother's organ in Ohrdruf was extensively rebuilt beginning while he lived there; and the St. Michael's organ in Lüneburg underwent broad repairs while he was a student there.[81] With his innate curiosity, Bach certainly made the most of these opportunities to learn about organs from the inside out.

Bach's contract "held him personally responsible for the use and condition of the organ. It admonished him to live uprightly, to fear God, to love peace, and to appear promptly at all rehearsals and services."[82] Bach's responsibilities amounted to playing for four services each week: Sunday at 8:00 a.m. for the main service; Monday at 7:00 a.m. for a prayer service; Wednesday at 2:00 p.m. for the vespers service; and Thursday at 7:00 a.m. for the early service.[83] His primary duties consisted of leading and accompanying the fifteen hundred congregants in the singing of chorales, playing chorale preludes to introduce the tunes, playing preludes and postludes at the beginning and end of the service, and supplying music during Communion.[84] With a relatively light schedule, a new instrument, and a paid bellows operator, Bach had significant time to compose, study, and practice.[85] In addition, Bach was under the care of a very able group of ministers who would have advanced his theological understanding and who cared deeply for quality church music.[86]

The only difficulty appeared to be responsibility concerning the rehearsing and directing of the student choir. Bach's contract did not specifically mention choir duties. The choir, consisting of boys nearly the same age as Bach, was poorly organized and had already gained a reputation for being disrespectful and unruly in church.[87] These rumbling conflicts erupted in August 1705 when the church consistory called Bach before them to answer questions about an altercation with a bassoon player named Geysersbach.

Apparently Bach insulted Johann Heinrich Geysersbach by calling him a "Zippel Fagottist" during a rehearsal, or "nanny-goat bassoonist." The phrase could also be translated from the Latin root in such a way to insinuate that Geysersbach was a pupil or novice, while Bach himself was above that status.[88] Either way, the fact that they were essentially the same age, with Geysersbach possibly as many as three years older, did not sit well with the instrumentalist. While coming home one night, Bach was accosted on the street by Geysersbach and his friends. Geysersbach carried a stick and told Bach that anyone who insulted his instrument insulted him. Bach drew his dagger, but Geysersbach took him to the ground. The two were separated before either one could seriously harm the other. The consistory admonished Bach that "men must live among *imperfecta;* he must get along with the students, and they must not make one another's lives miserable."[89]

A few months later, Bach requested, and was granted, four weeks' leave to travel the 250 miles to Lübeck to hear the music of the great German organist and composer Dietrich Buxtehude. Buxtehude started a tradition of a series of Sunday vesper services before the season of Advent, which became a tradition at St. Mary's Church for a generation.[90] In addition, Buxtehude presented two original oratorios in December with more than forty instrumentalists, choir, and organ in a genre, style, and manner of performance that would have been innovative and new to Bach.

Buxtehude incorporated a variety of styles, forms, and concepts in his work that included both ancient and contemporary ideas. In addition, his situation provided him with the opportunity to be the model of a scholar musician with freedom to develop his own projects, as well as the opportunity to play recitals and perform his own compositions, which set new standards for "form, size, texture, and character."[91] Bach must have been amazed and excited by what he was learning, because he extended his four-week absence to four months without a word of explanation to the church in Arnstadt or a request for an extension of his leave.

The impact of Buxtehude and his work on Bach was tremendous. "Just what he did in Lübeck is unknown; but that he absorbed much from Buxtehude's music is evident, especially in the dark richness of his later chromatic harmony; for Buxtehude's chromaticism was remarkable."[92] Buxtehude's compositions, use of instrumentalists, approach to performing, integration with the church liturgy, and the extent of performing and duties provided a model for Bach to aspire toward. Bach's reverence for Buxtehude continued throughout his life, and the most important transmission of Buxtehude's works in the eighteenth century occurred through the efforts of Bach and his circle of influence.[93]

Bach was offered Buxtehude's position while he was there. However attractive the offer might have been musically, it carried the traditional requirement that the successor marry an eligible daughter of the retiring organist. Buxtehude's daughter was unattractive and ten years older than the twenty-year-old Bach. He refused, just as Handel and Georg Philipp Telemann had done before him.[94]

One reason for Bach's refusal to accept the position as Buxtehude's successor could have been the presence of Maria Barbara, who was waiting back home in Arnstadt. Maria Barbara (1684–1720) was an orphan girl who moved into the Golden Crown Inn in Arnstadt in 1705. Coincidentally, the Golden Crown was where Bach lived, and Barbara's father had been a church organist.[95] Even more interesting was the fact that Barbara was a Bach, a distant cousin—they shared a great-grandfather.[96]

Bach returned from Lübeck by February 7, 1706, when he took Communion in Arnstadt. He spent the next two weeks trying to satisfy the angry church consistory as to the length of his absence. The consistory took this opportunity to continue to admonish Bach concerning his relationship with the students and the necessity of leading choir rehearsals.[97] He asked to be removed from the responsibility of choir duties, but he was reprimanded in writing to improve his relationship with the students.[98]

In addition, new complaints surfaced stemming from the performance of his duties. Bach returned to Arnstadt in February 1706 with "strong and clear convictions regarding music as an aid to worship."[99] Unfortunately, his personal maturity did not equal his musical and theological convictions. The consistory reproved him for adding and "mingling many strange" notes in the hymns and confusing the congregation in their singing and worship.[100] Bach apparently added embellishments and "played rather too long," to which the pastor called his attention; however, Bach reacted petulantly and "had at once fallen into the other extreme" and played too short.[101]

With new ideas and aims gathered from his time with Buxtehude, Bach knew he could never fulfill his ambitions in the hostile environment that had erupted in Arnstadt. His youth, inexperience, and immaturity exacerbated the situation beyond repair, and in the spring of 1707 he accepted another post as organist in Mühlhausen. On June 29, 1707, Bach appeared before the consistory and officially asked for his dismissal and returned the keys to the organ. Bach's cousin Johann Ernst Bach (from Ohrdruf and Hamburg days) was appointed as his successor—but at a reduced salary. Ernst had filled Bach's position during the four months he was away in Lübeck with Buxtehude.[102]

Despite his immaturity, Bach had utilized his time well at Arnstadt and had continued to develop his keyboard technique. Such that "already at twenty-two Bach seems to have acquired complete mastery of the problems of composition, and exhibits at the same time a sense of effect, both in the choral writing and in the instrumentation, which is altogether individual."[103] In subsequent positions, Bach had conflicts with his superiors; however, the nature of those conflicts was not the result of selfish immaturity or assertions of rights or privileges, but rather the responsible and wise reaction to attacks on biblical authority and the worship of God. Clearly Bach had learned his lessons well from his days in Arnstadt and grew because of them.

CLARIFICATION OF HIS CALLING
MÜHLHAUSEN, 1707–8

*His conscious life-long purpose was to enrich the
musical treasury of the Church he loved, to
strengthen and signalize every feature of her
worship which his genius could reach: and to this
lofty aim he devoted an intellectual force and an
energy of loyal enthusiasm unsurpassed in the
annals of art.*[104]

*O*N JULY 1, 1707, Johann Sebastian Bach began
his tenure as organist at St. Blasius's Church
in Mühlhausen. Located about thirty-six miles northwest
of Arnstadt, the city was governed by an elected council
of six aldermen and forty-two councillors.[105] Mühlhausen
was the second largest city in Thuringia after Erfurt. As an
imperial free city, Mühlhausen was one of only a few
cities independent of princely rule. Since the early thir-
teenth century, the city council had reported directly to
the emperor in Vienna.[106] This status as a free city lasted
from 1251 until 1803. As such, the position at St. Blasius's Church was a civic position, and Bach was a subject

of the city, which meant, for one thing, that he was not able to accept "professional engagements beyond the city limits without official sanction."[107]

Although he was only twenty-two years old, the council asked Bach to state his terms of employment. He requested and was granted the same salary he had at Arnstadt, plus certain perquisites, namely grain, wood, and kindling delivered to his door in addition to a wagon to move his belongings from Arnstadt.[108] There were thirteen churches in Mühlhausen, with St. Mary's and St. Blasius's Churches the largest and most important. The senior minister of the town taught primarily at St. Blasius, but tradition held that the ministers from these two churches alternated pulpits.[109]

The position that Bach filled had been vacant for six months before the council considered Bach for the job. He played his trial audition on Easter Sunday in April 1707. Soon afterward, a fire swept through the city that destroyed around four hundred buildings and approached the doorstep of the church.[110] As such, it was a subdued and wounded city in which Bach took up residence that July.

One source of happiness was no doubt his wedding to Maria Barbara on October 17, 1707. They married in the small neighboring village of Dornheim, with a friend of Barbara's family officiating. The fact that they married on a Monday enabled various guests to attend after leaving Sunday services the day before.[111]

As organist in Mühlhausen, Bach accompanied the congregational hymns as well as performed preludes, fugues, and chorale elaborations on all Sundays and feast days for the matins, morning, and afternoon services at St. Blasius's Church. In addition, he played for two services on Tuesday and Friday. Weddings and funerals were extra work and extra money.[112]

Every year in February a large municipal celebration took place for the outgoing council members and the newly elected councillors, in which "the Government of the Imperial Free City of Mühlhausen was joyously entrusted to the fatherly care of the new council."[113] The council requested that Bach provide a congratulatory vocal work in honor of the occasion. Bach befriended the pastor of St. Mary's Church, Georg Eilmer, who provided the lyrics for the cantata.[114] *Cantata* comes from the Latin word *cantare,* which means "to sing." Strictly speaking, the term designates a vocal work as opposed to an instrumental work, which would be called a *sonata* (from *sonare,* "to sound").[115]

The main pastor at St. Blasius's Church was strict about the use of music in the services. Therefore Bach had not had much opportunity to utilize and explore the ideas of liturgical music that he picked up from Buxtehude. However, St. Mary's Church was scheduled as the site for the performance of the celebratory cantata. Bach took advantage of this opportunity to write for a large ensemble, which included chorus and soloists as well as strings, woodwinds, trumpet fanfares, and tympani. The text was equally bold and epic, declaring "God is my King." The opening chorus addressed God as the heavenly King, and the closing chorus addressed Emperor Joseph as the reigning temporal king, thus making theological connections between the office and function of kingship. The cantata also included a duet for boy soprano and tenor, symbolizing youth and maturity as represented by the incoming and outgoing councilmen.[116]

This occasion was such a success that the council ordered the cantata be published in the city records—the only one of Bach's approximately three hundred cantatas that was published in his lifetime.[117] Also, two and a half weeks later Bach asked for and was granted an extensive repair project on the organ at St. Blasius's Church—another indication that Bach was highly regarded.

However, Bach requested to be dismissed from his post in June 1708. Bach had played for Duke Wilhelm of Weimar in the spring, and the duke had immediately offered Bach a position as court organist. As for Bach's reasons in desiring to leave Mühlhausen, he stated the following:

> Now God has so ordered it that a change has unexpectedly been put into my hands, in which I foresee the attainment of a more sufficient subsistence and the pursuit of my aims as regards the due ordering of church music without vexation from others, since his Royal and Serene Highness of Saxe-Weimar has graciously offered me the *entrée* to his Court Capelle and chamber music.[118]

Bach mentioned "hindrance" and "vexation" in his resignation letter; however, those terms need to be understood in the larger picture of what Bach now was determined to fulfill as his calling, the "ultimate goal, namely a well-regulated church music, to the Glory of God."[119] As Bach biographer Philipp Spitta explained:

We must understand in the first place the disposition of a portion of the municipality of Mühlhausen which clung to old fashions and customs, and neither could nor would follow Bach's bold flights, and even looked askance at the stranger who conducted himself so despotically in a position which, as far back as the memory of man extended, had always been filled by a native of the city, and for its sole honour and glory.[120]

A pupil of Bach later complained about the town "as a place where, as far as music was concerned, darkness covered the earth," and where there existed resistance to new ideas and improvements to the archaic system of organizing vocal and instrumental resources.[121]

Bach now clearly identified church music as his ultimate goal and aim. He wanted to direct his talents in composition and performing for "well-regulated church music to the glory of God."[122] He had exhausted the available opportunities in Mühlhausen and needed a place where he could have additional prospects in following this calling. Bach handled this situation of his leaving so well and left on such good terms that the council asked him to compose the celebratory cantatas for the next two years and to come back and perform them. Also, Bach continued to supervise the rebuilding of the organ as he had outlined and specified. In his now-vacant position, Bach left his cousin Johann Friedrich Bach (c. 1682–1730), who served St. Blasius's Church until his death. In addition, in 1735 Bach helped his third son, Johann Gottfried Bernhard, secure the appointment as organist at St. Mary's Church.

In addition to valuable experience and a significant

increase in his stature as a musician, Bach's letter of resignation indicated that he had "acquired from far and
wide, not without cost, a good store of the choicest
church compositions."[123] Despite the fact that he was
only in Mühlhausen a year, those twelve months proved
to be a pivotal time in his development as an artist and as
a mature person.

HONOR AND STABILITY
WEIMAR: 1708–14

Perfectly constructed and unique in sound, Bach's compositions offer the ideal of bringing into congruence original thought, technical exactitude, and aesthetic beauty.[124]

JOHANN NIKOLAUS FORKEL SUCCINCTLY summed up Bach's tenure at Weimar in his 1802 biography of the composer.

[When Bach] made a journey to Weimar to perform before the reigning Duke, his performance on the organ was so highly approved of that he was offered the place of Court Organist, which he accepted. The extended sphere of action for his art in which he here lived, impelled him to try out everything possible in this art; and this was actually the period during which he not only made himself so able a performer on the organ, but also laid the foundation of his great body of compositions for that instrument. He had still further occasion to improve in his art when his Prince, in 1717, appointed him Concertmeister, in which office he had also to compose and execute pieces of sacred music.[125]

In 1708 Duke Wilhelm Ernst hired Bach as court organist; it was Wilhelm's younger brother who had employed Bach as a violinist back in 1703. Wilhelm offered Bach twice his salary at Mühlhausen and included an allotment of coal to heat the chapel so that he could practice during the winter months.[126] In addition to his salary, Bach also received eighteen bushels of wheat, twelve bushels of barley, four cords of firewood, and thirty pails of tax-free beer each year.[127]

Bach and his pregnant wife, Barbara, moved into an apartment located on the market square sometime before July 14, 1708. The dwelling was reserved for court employees and was only a five-minute walk from the Wilhelmsburg, the ducal palace. In addition to their first child, Catharina Dorothea, born on December 29, 1708, their household swelled with the inclusion of Barbara's older unmarried sister (who lived with the family from 1709 until her death in 1729) and two students who had moved with them from Mühlhausen. Over time they were joined by a succession of more than ten other students, including Bach's nephew, the second son of his brother Christoph, providing Bach an opportunity to repay his brother's kindness to him as a child.[128] Barbara bore six of her seven children in Weimar, two of whom died in infancy.

Weimar had a population of around five thousand, of which almost one-third were directly or indirectly employed by the court. More than fifty thousand people lived in the entire duchy under the co-regents of the Ernestine-Saxon dynasty. Duke Wilhelm lived in the Wilhelmsburg, a massive palace built in the 1650s, and his nephew and coruler, Ernst Augustus, lived in the nearby Red Palace. Wilhelm was the dominant ruler, but there were various power struggles between the co-regents. Wilhelm was a deeply religious man and a music lover very fond of the organ. He employed only Lutheran servants and insisted that they attend all chapel services. His personal life consisted of "daily devotions, exemplary demeanor, and substantial benefactions both to individuals and institutions."[129]

Wilhelm held Bach in high esteem, but it was Ernst Augustus with whom Bach had a personal friendship. Ernst Augustus played the violin and trumpet and collected musical instruments and musical scores.[130] It was his father who had reassembled the court *capelle* over a period of many years. Some of the power struggles between uncle and nephew concerned the court musicians, since they were considered to be joint servants. In 1707 Wilhelm decreed that his permission was required in order for court musicians to make music at the Red Palace. Additional conflicts included Wilhelm's arresting Ernst Augustus's councillors at one point, and Ernst Augustus's assuming total control in 1728.[131]

Although Bach also played in the court *capelle,* or orchestra, his principal responsibility was as church organist for the palace church, which was attended by the ducal families, members of the princely household, other gentry, court officials, and select employees. The palace church was approximately one hundred feet long by forty feet wide, with a total height of ninety feet. The overall effect was of its being narrow and tall with two galleries and walls that extended upward for three floors.[132] One of the most striking features was the location of the organ and musicians. "Cut into the flat ceiling of the sanctuary (about 65 feet above the floor level) was a wide rectangular aperture—about 13 by 10 feet and surrounded by a balustrade—that opened into the music gallery, a spacious domed compartment called the *Capelle*."[133] The balustrade served as a music stand so that the sounds of music came from above as if descending from heaven.

Bach's work obviously pleased Duke Wilhelm, because he increased Bach's salary in June 1711 by 25 percent and augmented his additional allowances after only three years' employment. Bach's salary now equaled that of his superior, Capellmeister Samuel Drese, who had worked for the duke thirty-three years at the same salary without any pay raise.[134]

In February 1713 the court of Saxe-Weissenfels commissioned Bach to compose a festive cantata in honor of Duke Christian's thirty-first birthday. Bach presented the "Hunt" Cantata at a banquet held at the hunting lodges after the completion of the chase. It was such a complete success that the piece was repeated in 1716. Bach's association with Duke Christian extended for many years after the duke bestowed the title of capellmeister on Bach in 1729. Three days after the birthday celebration, Duke Wilhelm immediately increased Bach's salary again to a level above that of Samuel Drese.[135]

In 1714 there was yet another change in Bach's position within the court. The official decree read:

On Friday, March 2, 1714, His Serene Highness the
Reigning Duke most graciously conferred upon the quon-
dam Court Organist Bach, at his most humble request,
the title of Concertmaster, with official rank below that of
Vice-Capellmeister Drese, for which he is to be obliged to
perform new works monthly. And for rehearsals of those,
the musicians of the capelle are required to appear upon
his demand.[136]

Bach was given the newly formed title of concertmaster; however, it was explicitly stated that the hierarchy of
the lead musicians remain the same, with Bach still behind
Capellmeister Drese and Vice-Capellmeister Wilhelm
Drese, his son, despite the fact that he continued to be
paid more. Bach's responsibilities as concertmaster included leading the players, usually by the playing of the
lead violin part, and all technical aspects of the performance, from making up the ensemble, organizing rehearsals,
positioning players, and conducting performances. The
first thing Bach did was to move rehearsals to the music
gallery in order to maintain tighter control over rehearsals.[137] Duke Wilhelm's move might have been
prompted by a job offer that Bach received from a church
in Halle early in 1714. Whatever the reason, Bach was
now in a position to pursue his desire to compose new
music for worship services according to a monthly schedule that alternated with Samuel and Wilhelm Drese.[138] As
Christoph Wolff wrote, the decision of 1714 "grew out of
deep-rooted drive to commit musical thought to paper, to
think about and embark on their further elaboration, to refine the technical skills necessary for the theoretical

underpinnings and compositional control of the musical substance at hand, and constantly to challenge his musical imagination."[139]

March 1714 saw the commencement of a cycle of cantatas for well-regulated church music. Bach was one step closer to his calling and goal.

INTERLUDE
MUSIC FOR ORGAN

*To enumerate the organ works of the early Weimar
years would be to list the bulk of Bach's output in
that field. Preludes, fugues, toccatas, and chorale
preludes issued from his pen in great profusion.*[140]

BACH'S OBITUARY MENTIONS HIS time in Weimar
by saying, "The pleasure His Grace took in
his playing fired him with the desire to try every possible
artistry in his treatment of the organ. Here, too, he wrote
most of his organ works. . . . In Weymar he also trained
various competent organists."[141] For the first six years
Bach was in Weimar, his primary responsibility was that of
organist to the court. The statement above suggests that
in true Bach fashion, he expanded the expectations of his
position and took full advantage of the opportunities before him to compose and to perform.

During his tenure at the court in Weimar around the
age of twenty-five, Bach reached the point of full technical
facility at the keyboard—a skill he merely sought to refine
further over subsequent years.[142]

Bach's obituary also gave an indication of his abilities
when it said:

Bach not only understood the art of playing the organ, of combining the various stops of that instrument in the most skillful manner, and of displaying each stop according to its character in the greatest perfection, but he also knew the construction of organs from one end to the other. . . . No one could draw up or judge dispositions for new organs better than he.[143]

The organ was the largest and most complex machine in Germany from the sixteenth to the eighteenth centuries. Knowledge of the organ to this degree "embodied [the] science of mechanical engineering, physics (acoustics), chemistry (metallurgy), and mathematics as well as architecture and the handicraft of carpentry and plumbing."[144] The organ itself comprised "a myriad of individual parts using all sorts of metal, wood, leather, ivory, cloth, and other materials. Its combination of wind chests, bellows, ranks of pipes, and keyboards was capable of producing colorful sonorities of different dynamic ranges, whose spectrum and volume depended on the size of the instrument."[145]

Students and witnesses attested to his proficiency in playing by saying that "with his two feet, he could play things on the pedals" that other skilled players could not play with their hands,[146] that he understood the various sounds of the organ stops so well that he would write with specific sounds and combination of sounds in mind,[147] and that he understood the nature of the organ to such a degree that the types of music and melodies he played and wrote on the organ were different from the music he executed on other keyboard instruments.[148] In other words, he was able to make the most of the unique abilities of every instrument through his profound knowledge of the strengths of each. This was most certainly true with regard to his organ music for church. As Forkel wrote:

> To play properly on the organ, the character of the ideas which the organist employs must be of primary import. This character is determined by the nature of the instrument, by the place in which it stands, and, lastly, by the object proposed. . . . The purpose of the organ to support church singing, and to prepare and maintain devout feeling by preludes and postludes, requires further that the composition and connection of the tones be effected in a different manner from which is practiced out of the church. The common, the trite can never become solemn, can never excite a sublime feeling; it must, therefore, in every respect be banished from the organ.[149]

Bach's organ works can essentially be divided into two types: those based on chorale, or hymn, melodies; and those that are "free" compositions, independent of chorales.[150] Some of these works bear mentioning.

The *Orgel-Büchlein* (Little Organ Book) is a composition collection that spanned the entire Weimar years. Bach planned to include 164 chorales for use by church organists. The first fifty-five were harmonizations of the hymn of the day for each Sunday and feast day, following the church calendar starting with Advent and concluding with Trinity Sunday. The remainder of the entries specifically illustrated aspects of the Christian life.[151] Bach's intent for the book was outlined on the title page: "Little

Organ Book, In which a beginner at the organ is given instruction in developing a chorale in many divers ways,
and at the same time in acquiring facility in the study of
the pedal since in the chorales contained therein the pedal
is treated as wholly *obbligato* [essential, not optional]." He
concluded with a rhyming couplet:

> In praise of the Almighty's will
> And for my neighbor's greater skill.[152]

There are more than 125 chorale preludes that still
exist from Bach's fertile imagination. "The chorals that
were appointed for the day would commonly furnish the
player with his raw material, and the song of the people
would appear again soaring above their heads, adorned by
effective tonal combinations."[153] In the chorale preludes
the melody of the hymn remained unchanged. Bach used
these familiar tunes as a *cantus firmus,* or foundational
music line, around which he added freely invented parts
that were intertwined with the tune.[154] Bach brought the
organ chorale and prelude to a height of artistic perfection.

Other works from this period in the free style include a
variety of preludes, fugues, toccatas, and passacaglia—all
various forms on which Bach built the structure of his
grand musical ides.

"In a word, his great genius, which comprehended
everything and united everything requisite to the perfection of one of the most inexhaustible arts, brought the art
of the organ, too, to a degree of perfection which it never
attained before his time and will hardly ever attain
again."[155]

Development and Disappointment
Weimar: 1714–17

Bach's adaptation, integration, and command of both modern and traditional compositional approaches represent a systematic attempt at shaping and perfecting his personal musical language and expanding its structural possibilities and expressive powers.[156]

AFTER HIS PROMOTION IN 1714, Bach's position enabled him to regularly contribute to the writing of church cantatas on the schedule of one each month. He rotated in the writing schedule with Capellmeister Samuel Drese and Vice-Capellmeister Wilhelm Drese. With a salary greater than either one of his superiors and now the opportunity to do some of the work associated with the position, surely Bach hoped for the opportunity of ascending to the position of capellmeister in the eventuality of the aged Drese's death. "The ultimate goal for an aspiring instrumentalist was the post of Kapellmeister, the person charged with directing the music, both sacred and secular, of an entire court, and usually expected to compose as well."[157]

There are approximately twenty cantatas extant from the Weimar period, but Bach must have written at least twice as many.[158] These cantatas, written between 1713 and 1716, appear to be a systematic exploration of various compositional possibilities with regard to "genre, form, technique, scoring, and texture on the broader level, and metric-rhythm patterns, key choices, thematic treatment, and harmonic designs on the narrower."[159] In other words, Bach was making the most of his opportunity to try new ideas to stretch himself as a composer and to stretch the notion of a cantata. In addition to these technical and minute elements of the compositional art, Bach also started matching his "fluent and increasing[ly] complex musical language with the structured prose and poetry" of the lyrics for the cantatas.[160] These lyrics, or librettos, were a combination of biblical passages or verses, modern poetic verse, and well-known chorale texts.

An important element at this stage in Bach's development as a composer was his conscious exposure and study of Italian music. As Donald Grout wrote:

He studied the music of other composers through the customary method of copying or arranging their scores, a habit which he retained all through his life. In this way he became familiar with the styles of the foremost composers of France, Germany, Austria, and Italy, assimilating the characteristic excellences of each. . . . The natural consequence of these studies was an important change in Bach's own style: from the Italians, especially Vivaldi, he learned to write more concise themes, to clarify and tighten the harmonic scheme, and above all to develop subjects by a continuous rhythmic flow into lucid, grandly proportioned, formal structures.[161]

Duke Wilhelm had a large library of Italian music, which was available for Bach to study.[162] Studying, copying, and arranging the music of Vivaldi enabled Bach to assimilate ideas of "order, connection, and proportion" into his musical ideas and to teach him to "think musically."[163] Vivaldi's music had a foundation in two aesthetic premises: "Simplicity (implying a broad spectrum from purity, clarity, and correctness to graceful and natural elegance) and complexity (implying intellectual analysis, sophisticated elaboration, and rational control)."[164] It was this paradoxical element that Bach continued to explore and achieve throughout the rest of his life—resulting in works that are easily accessible yet learned.

In addition to his duties in the church services, Bach also participated in a rich and varied musical life—especially in an abundance of musical activities in the Red Palace. Bach enjoyed a close personal relationship with the musical Duke Ernst Augustus and his younger half brother, Prince Johann Ernst. Most likely the two of them joined in the festivities, since they both played multiple instruments. These musical activities annoyed Duke Wilhelm to the extent that he forbade any of the court musicians to engage in musical activities at the adjoining Red Palace under pain of fine and arrest.[165]

Bach ignored these unreasonable demands from Duke Wilhelm and, in January 1716, joined in the wedding ceremony of Duke Ernst Augustus, most likely writing the wedding cantata, for which only the text remains.[166] The bride, Princess Elenore Wilhelmine, was the sister of Prince Leopold of Anhalt-Cöthen. A few months later, in April 1716, Ernst Augustus celebrated his twenty-eighth birthday with a performance of Bach's "Hunt" Cantata. Prince Leopold was most assuredly present at some if not all of these occasions and heard Bach's music.[167]

On December 1, 1716, Samuel Drese, the capell-meister since 1683, died. For the next three Sundays in Advent, Bach took over the writing of the weekly church cantatas.[168] Duke Wilhelm and Duke Ernst Augustus were at odds as to how to fill the vacant position. Despite the fact that Bach was more than qualified, had proved himself musically and as a political asset, and had in essence been doing part of the job of capellmeister already, Wilhelm presumably wanted to punish him for his friendship with his nephew and the flaunting of his demands. They sought the services of an outside candidate, Georg Philipp Telemann, but he refused the post. The duke wanted to offer the position to Wilhelm Drese, who had served under his father as vice-capellmeister since 1704.[169]

Ernst Augustus convinced his brother-in-law, Prince Leopold of Saxe-Cöthen, to hire Bach as his capellmeister as compensation to Bach.[170] In early August 1717 Bach traveled the sixty miles to Cöthen and signed an agreement accepting the post. The prince offered him a salary one-third more than Bach had received in his position at Weimar.[171] However, in retaliation for the interference from the Red Palace, Duke Wilhelm refused to release Bach from his service.

Around this same time, Bach journeyed to Dresden to play before the king in a keyboard challenge against the boastful Frenchman Marchand. Marchand accepted the challenge but then slipped out of town early in the morning before the competition scheduled to take place later that day. Bach then played before the king and the court to much acclaim. Bach's status and reputation continued to rise in ever-greater spheres.

When Bach returned to Weimar, the situation remained unresolved as Duke Wilhelm continued to obstinately refuse to release Bach for the position in Cöthen. Finally Wilhelm had had enough and put Bach in jail. As the official court secretary's report reads:

> On November 6, [1717,] the quondam [erstwhile] concertmaster and organist Bach was confined to the County Judge's place of detention for too stubbornly forcing the issue of his dismissal and finally on December 2 was freed from arrest with notice of his unfavorable discharge.[172]

Most likely Bach used these almost four weeks of imprisonment to write music. Whatever the case, what started as a venue with great promise and opportunity to pursue the writing of "well-regulated church music" for the glory of God ended with an embittered relationship and an "unfavorable discharge."

Johann Wilhelm Drese was promoted to capellmeister, and Bach's student who had followed him from Mühlhausen, Johann Martin Schubart, was appointed chamber musician and court organist, both on January 5, 1718. The positions of vice-capellmeister and concertmaster remained vacant.[173] Bach and his family set out for Cöthen and a new beginning.

DEVIATION FROM CALLING
CÖTHEN: 1717–23

> *Here he . . . devoted himself almost wholly to the*
> *composition of instrumental music. . . . The*
> *smaller keyboard instruments, the violin, the*
> *violoncello, the flute, and the orchestra are all*
> *studied in their minutest detail; it might almost be*
> *said that the foundations of modern instrumental*
> *literature were laid by Bach during his six years'*
> *residence at Cöthen.*[174]

*I*N DECEMBER 1717 BACH, Barbara, and their four children, ages nine to two, moved to Cöthen along with Barbara's sister Friedelena. Their rented apartment was spacious and conveniently located near the main gate of the palace. Cöthen had a population of about three thousand, with the entire surrounding agrarian region totaling only around ten thousand.[175] The principal mail and coach line from Hamburg to Leipzig ran through Cöthen, and because of its rural and rustic environment, it was dubbed "Cow Cöthen."[176] Prince Leopold highly regarded his new capellmeister, and Bach was one of the highest-paid court officials in the entire principality, with an elite and professional instrumental ensemble under his direction. Leopold gave Bach a great deal of personal support in his work.[177]

Prince Leopold was only ten years old when he acceded to the throne, but as a minor, he was placed under the guardianship of his mother, Princess Gisela Agnes, who ruled in his stead. Agnes was a devout Lutheran who had married a staunch Calvinist. As such, she sought to better the conditions of her fellow Lutherans by building a Lutheran church and a Lutheran school (where Bach's children attended) and by establishing a foundation for Lutheran girls and women of gentle birth. "While she ruled with considerable wisdom, political prudence, and a strong sense of equity and social justice, she also kept a firm grip on everything that would benefit the largely underprivileged Lutherans."[178]

At the time of Bach's appointment in Cöthen, Prince Leopold was twenty-three years old (nine years younger than Bach) and a bachelor. Leopold played several stringed instruments and the clavier, and he possessed a good bass-baritone voice. He accepted Bach as a personal friend and traveling companion and even stood as godfather to Bach's son born in Cöthen (Leopold Augustus, b. November 1718; d. September 1719).[179]

Music was an important part of Leopold's life. When he was a young teenager, he was skilled enough on the bass viol that he persuaded his mother to engage three other musicians at court so that they could play chamber music together.[180] Leopold attended the Ritteracademie in Berlin, one of the premier schools for princes in Germany. He then embarked on a grand tour, which included the Hague and Amsterdam in the Netherlands, England,

Germany, France, and Italy—where he spent three months in Rome. He returned by way of Florence, Venice, Vienna, Prague, Dresden, and Leipzig. Along the way he acquired published music and took a composer along with him on his travels.[181]

In 1713 Friedrich Wilhelm I of Prussia, the "Soldier King," dissolved the court *capelle* in Berlin after he rose to power. Leopold heard about this action and convinced his mother to hire a core group of experienced players for his own court *capelle* in Cöthen. When Bach entered his position, he already had an ensemble of sixteen experienced members—many of whom were on the virtuoso level.[182] Various players and singers would also join the *capelle* for special performances.

Bach entered a highly productive time of instrumental composing. Because of the religious nature of the court, no sacred music was required of him, and there was never a full complement of singers.[183] Because there are great gaps in the works of Bach that survived, it is impossible to know all that he wrote during this time period; however, several clues suggest a prodigious output. The *capelle* kept a music copyist on salary and even paid for an additional copyist from 1719 to 1721, indicating that there was a need for two people to copy all of the many parts and music scores necessary for performances. In addition, the music budget for book binding was sufficient to bind the score and parts of roughly one new work a week of medium size. This continued output would represent some 350 pieces for chamber and orchestral ensembles as well as serenades and vocal works.[184]

Under the patronage of a supportive and gracious

prince with whom he had a great personal relationship, Bach flourished with the synergy of writing for professional players and had considerable time to spend on his pursuits.[185]

In May 1720, for the second time, Prince Leopold left for the spa at Carlsbad in northwestern Bohemia for health reasons. Bach and several other musicians accompanied him—the first time he took seven musicians and a keyboard. They remained at the fashionable spa for more than a month.[186] Bach left Maria Barbara and their four children at home.[187] When Bach returned to Cöthen on July 27, he was greeted with the news that his wife Barbara had died on July 2 and was buried before they could send him news.[188] His oldest son, Wilhelm Friedemann, was nine years old—the same age Bach was when he lost his mother.

Bach's deep sorrow at the death of his first wife is perhaps manifested in the music he played and wrote in the following months. Despite his lucrative and fulfilling position with Prince Leopold of Saxe-Cöthen, Bach played an audition for a position as organist in Hamburg. It was on this occasion that he had the opportunity to play for the ninety-seven-year-old organ master, Reinken, who had encouraged him twenty years before. One of the pieces Bach played was a half-hour-long improvisation on the chorale tune "By the Waters of Babylon,"[189] which comes from Psalm 137:1: "By the waters of Babylon, there we sat down and wept." In addition, the cantata he presented in November of that year was based on the chorale "I had much distress in my heart, but your consolation restores my soul."

Bach remained the top candidate for the job in Hamburg, despite the fact that he officially withdrew from the process. Bach might have withdrawn because of the expected bribe associated with obtaining the position. The candidate who succeeded in securing the position subsequently made a sizable donation to the church.

Several other significant events occurred around this time. In the fall of 1719, George Frideric Handel visited the Continent to engage singers for the first opera season of the new Royal Academy in London. He stayed for a time with family in Halle—just twenty miles from Cöthen. Bach attempted to go and meet him; however, he was told that Handel had just left. In February 1721 Bach's older brother, Johann Christoph, died in Ohrdruf. It was Christoph who had cared for Bach as an orphaned child. In March 1721 Bach completed the composition of the six *Brandenburg Concertos*—a masterpiece of variety and a virtuoso display of writing and performance.[190]

On December 3, 1721, Bach remarried. His wife was a professional singer by the name of Anna Magdalena Wülken, who was sixteen years younger than he was and from a musical family.[191] The first mention of the two of them is in a church register in which they are jointly acting as godparents to the son of Leopold's butler. Magdalena was described as "a court singer here," indicating that they must have known each other.

Just eight days later, Prince Leopold married nineteen-year-old Friederica Henrietta, a princess of Anhalt-Bernberg.[192] From that point on there was a steady decline in the attitude toward the arts in Cöthen, and Bach later described Leopold's wife as *amusa,* or against the arts. From 1717 to 1720, Leopold had increased the court music budget annually, but after his marriage, the budget declined (6 percent one year and 9 percent another). Membership in the *capelle* decreased through attrition and death, but members were not replaced by new players. One player was replaced, not by another musician, but by a dancing instructor. Several extravagant expenditures and tightening revenues caused Leopold to need extra money.[193]

In addition, conditions worsened at the Lutheran school Bach's children attended. There were teacher shortages, overcrowded classrooms, and an administrator with questionable abilities and morals. All of these elements indicated to Bach that he needed to find another location for suitable employment.

Forty miles away, in Leipzig, the cantor of the St. Thomas School died in June 1722, after almost forty years of being active in the musical life of that city. The council was divided between wanting a good cantor who could teach academic subjects at the school and wanting a gifted musician and composer as a music director for the sake of the school, church, and broader community. In August 1722 the council elected Georg Philipp Telemann as cantor, but his authorities in Hamburg would not release him. The council's second choice, Johann Christoph Graupner, was offered the position in January 1723, but he too was unable to secure his release. Bach performed his trial audition on February 7, 1723. After much discussion and debate, the council finally decided to offer him the post in late April.[194] As one of the councillors said at the time, "As we were not able to obtain the best, we had to take the mediocre."[195]

One month later, with Leopold's good wishes, Sebastian, Magdalena, and their household arrived in Leipzig for what would be a twenty-seven-year employment with profound achievements but aggravating circumstances.

INTERLUDE
INSTRUMENTAL MUSIC

Individually and collectively, Bach's works demonstrate the musical realization of unity in diversity, or musical perfection.[196]

*W*ITH THE OPPORTUNITY AND necessary resources, Bach entered into a fruitful time of composition during his years in Cöthen. In addition to newly composed works, Bach was able to complete several collections of pieces that he had started compiling through the years. Specifically worthy of mention are *The Well-Tempered Clavier,* the *Orgel-Büchlein* (Little Organ Book), the *Brandenburg Concertos,* and the solo works for violin and cello.

"A Bach composition must be followed both horizontally and vertically."[197] While flowing over a firm chordal progression and foundation, the lines in Bach's music intertwine with one another in an interplay of ideas and techniques.

Undoubtedly the best-known of Bach's clavier works is the famous set of preludes and fugues called *The Well-Tempered Clavier.* Part 1 was completed at Cöthen in

1722, and part 2 was collected at Leipzig around 1740. Each part consists of twenty-four preludes and fugues, one prelude and one fugue in each of the twelve major and minor keys.[198] In addition to illustrating the concept of equal tuning, these works were designed by Bach for the purpose of teaching; most of the preludes have a single technical task given to the player.[199] Because of this, there is an astonishing variety of styles and moods exhibited in each of the pieces. "No two are alike, and each develops for the most part from a germinal idea stated in its opening bar."[200]

The word *fugue* comes from the Latin word *fuga,* or "flight." In a fugue, the primary melody idea, or subject, moves from voice to voice. Because there is melody present in each of the voice parts, each line deserves attention—especially the inner voices below the soprano, or highest, line. "There are chord progressions, of course, but they are a byproduct of independent strands of melody in simultaneous presentation."[201]

The *Orgel-Büchlein* (Little Organ Book) was a planned collection of 164 titles that Bach only partially finished. The plan was to present a harmonization of each of the hymns of the day for each Sunday and feast day. The other entries were hymns that dealt with various aspects of the Christian life. "Each prelude is a miniature tone poem developed from a basic programmatic idea."[202]

The *Brandenburg Concertos* offer a wealth of innovative techniques, creative use of instruments, and demanding virtuoso playing.[203] They contain a great breadth of "variety in instrumentation[,] and the thematic development is phenomenal."[204] Bach once again combined diversity with unity. The music itself looks incredibly complex on the page, "yet, in performance, a contagious pulse, a melodic naïveté, and harmonic simplicity override the trammels of technique to reach to all who are sensitive to the elements of rhythm, harmony, and melody."[205]

With the solo works for violin and cello, "once again, Bach the quintessential instrumentalist raises and redefines the technical standards of performing by fully exploring the idiomatic qualities of the violin and cello."[206] Both of these sets of pieces are compositions for unaccompanied instruments; in other words, a single player. These works display Bach's ability to convey "defined harmony" and "dense counterpoint" through a single statement of complex melody lines.[207]

Reflecting but a fraction of his total compositions during this period, each of these works defined the very nature of what it set out to accomplish. These works are the epitome of keyboard preludes and fugues, organ chorales, instrumental concertos, and solo works. The amazing feat was that Bach was able to reach the summit of very different genres with complete skill, artistry, and expertise.

THE EARLY YEARS IN LEIPZIG
1720s

*His conscious life-long purpose was to enrich the
musical treasury of the Church he loved, to
strengthen and signalize every feature of her
worship which his genius could reach: and to this
lofty aim he devoted an intellectual force and an
energy of loyal enthusiasm unsurpassed in the
annals of art.[208]*

LEIPZIG, MAY 29, 1723: This past Saturday afternoon, four
wagons loaded with household goods arrived here from
Cöthen; they belonged to the former Princely Capellmeister there, now called to Leipzig as Cantor Figuralis.
He himself arrived with his family on 2 carriages at 2
o'clock and moved into the newly renovated apartment
in the St. Thomas School.[209]

*T*HUS THE HAMBURG NEWSPAPER announced the
arrival of the Bach household to Leipzig: Sebastian, Anna Magdalena, Bach's late wife's sister, Friedelena Margaretha Bach, and five children, including the
newborn Christiana Sophia Henrietta—Magdalena's firstborn. Sadly, the new baby died around her third birthday.[210]

The apartment extended over three floors in the south wing of the St. Thomas School. In addition to the living quarters, it contained the cantor's office, the so-called composing room, and the school library. The dwelling also had direct access to the school, which was convenient for not only Bach, but also Friedemann (age twelve) and Carl Philipp Emanuel (age nine), who were accepted as non-resident students in the respective *tertia* and *quinta* classes. Their younger brothers followed them in subsequent years. Bach's annual salary amounted to slightly more than one-fourth his previous wages in Cöthen, but he did receive free housing, payments for light and heat, and supplemental endowments. However, the incidental income turned out to be much less than he had been led to believe he would receive.[211]

At the time that Bach moved, Leipzig was a large commercial town of about thirty thousand inhabitants. Second only to Dresden as the most important city in Saxony, Leipzig was known for its publishing and book trade, its prestigious university (founded in 1409), and its regular trade fairs.[212] Leipzig's origin dated back to an old Slavic settlement called Lipsk, meaning "the place of the linden trees." The city was charted between 1156 and 1170 and grew into a commercial center due to its location at the intersection of trade routes that literally spread throughout the rest of Europe. By 1458, regular trade fairs were held three times a year for a week to ten days each. These fairs were the New Year's Fair starting on January 1, the Easter or Jubilate Fair in the spring (beginning on Jubilate Sunday, the third Sunday after Easter), and the St. Michael's Fair in the fall (beginning on the Sunday after

St. Michael's Day—September 29). Six to ten thousand people would come for the fairs to the "marketplace of Europe."[213]

The citizens of Leipzig had a desire to make their town a center for the performing and visual arts. Residents put forth great effort in architecture and in the building of elaborate parks, hot houses, orangeries, and lodges outside the city walls. There was also an interest in art collecting, with the grandest collection belonging to Johann Christoph Richter, who had accumulated four hundred works by Titian, Raphael, Rubens, and others. On Wednesday from 2:00 to 4:00 p.m., visitors could see Gottfried Winckler's collection for free—which included paintings by Leonardo, Giorgione, Veronese, Tintoretto, Rubens, Hals, Brueghel, and Rembrandt.[214]

Inherent in the city was the tension between being progressive and cosmopolitan or proudly displaying the best of Germany's efforts without apology. Bach got caught in the cross fire of this struggle as certain leaders sought to adopt the secular elements of the Enlightenment.

Bach's official title was *Cantor et Director Musices,* meaning that he functioned as the cantor of St. Thomas School, within which capacity he was the music director as well, responsible for the music in the four city churches.[215] The position of cantor, by definition, was "a position which usually combined overall responsibility for the music of a church with a senior post at the local school."[216] The students Bach taught at the school were responsible for providing the music at the city's churches each Sunday. This concept was a conscious part of Martin Luther's agenda during the Reformation: "Luther did not destroy the choral tradition of the medieval school system but modified it and insisted that the teaching of music in these schools should have a primary importance, since they nourished and promoted the music of the church."[217] Luther wrote, "Music I have always loved. He who knows music has a good nature. Necessity demands that music be kept in the schools. A schoolmaster must be able to sing; otherwise I will not look at him. And before a young man is ordained in the ministry, he should practice music in school."[218]

Initially founded in 1212 as an Augustine choir school, St. Thomas School transformed into a Lutheran academy after the Reformation came through Leipzig in 1527 and Luther preached at St. Thomas Church. In addition to students from the town, the school provided accommodations for fifty-six boarding students called "alumni," who formed the basis of the choir forces. "The special role of music in St. Thomas school can be seen in the fact that almost half of the rules for accepting new pupils were aimed at ensuring that the pupils had sufficiently musical gifts"; as such, new students had to possess musical knowledge or aptitude and be able to "perform a piece completely and properly."[219]

Bach's specific duties at the school involved teaching music and other subjects to the upper school boarders and giving private lessons and tutoring as needed. Private instrumental lessons and keyboard instruction were part of Bach's daily routine with students, and most resident students had access to their own keyboards in their study cubicles.[220] This schedule included the preparation of the choirs for the church services in town, directing the primary chorus at the two main churches on alternate Sundays, oversight of the organists and other musicians, and bearing responsibility for instruments and performance materials. Every fourth week, Bach had to act as school inspector and take full responsibility for the students, including waking them up in the morning (5:00 a.m. in summer and 6:00 a.m. in winter), saying prayers fifteen minutes later, supervising meals, taking responsibility for school discipline, and making sure everybody got to bed at lights-out.[221] Maintaining school discipline involved assessing fines for misbehavior, including:

> For losing the key or leaving it in the door;
> For failing to shut the door when the last to leave a room;
> For being sick (*qui vomitat*);
> For swearing, loud, or improper speech;
> For impertinent language, in Latin or German;
> For not getting up in the morning and missing prayers;
> For not tidying cubicle before 10 in summer and 12 in winter.[222]

All teaching of students was to be for the purpose of instructing them "in the knowledge and fear of God" and "in the vivid knowledge of divine essence and will."[223]

Because of the arrangement of his various duties, Bach was under the authority of three separate entities. His immediate supervisor was the rector of the school; as cantor, he ranked third in the hierarchy of school officials. Bach was also subject to the civil authority of the municipal council and the ecclesiastical authority vested in the church consistory, the governing body of the congregation.[224] Bach's title of *director musices* required him to provide music for civic occasions (celebrations for the election of new officials, visiting dignitaries, etc.) and "to supervise the church music of the city as a whole."[225]

The two main churches were St. Nicholas (the official town church until 1755) and St. Thomas.[226] The students were divided into four choirs, with the best and most experienced students making up the choirs that sang at St. Thomas and St. Nicholas and having greater responsibilities. Bach directed the primary choir, which presented a cantata each week, alternating between the two churches. The weekly services required the singing of a cantata, a choral motet, several chorales, and the *Kyrie* and *Gloria*. The churches required additional special music at Christmas and Easter, Passion music on Good Friday, and various pieces for funerals, weddings, and civic events.[227] The principal church service lasted from 7:00 to 11:00 a.m., followed by another service beginning at 1:00 p.m. for vespers.[228] The choir sang the cantata at one church in the morning and again at the other church during the vespers service in the afternoon.

Bach set out on an astonishing mission to compose new cantatas for the worship services on a weekly basis. "In the course of two and a half years, Bach composed almost 150 church cantatas."[229] He was finally in a situation to enact his stated vocational calling of providing well-regulated church music. Bach's goal was to write five cycles of cantatas based on the principal chorales assigned to each Sunday and feast day throughout the church year. To this end, he wrote some 295 cantatas, thus providing him with a wealth of music for subsequent years as the cycles repeated. Each cantata was twenty to sixty minutes in length and provided a musical sermon that highlighted the Gospel reading and hymn for each Sunday.

In addition, Bach set out to compose a series of Passions based on the different Gospel accounts of the death of Christ. The choir sang these works as part of a long-standing tradition for Good Friday services. For his first Good Friday in Leipzig (1724), Bach wrote the *St. John Passion*. After heavy revision, it was performed again in 1725. Apparently, Bach performed the *St. Matthew Passion* in 1727 and again in 1729. It reached its final form in 1736.[230] As music historian Donald Grout wrote, "The culmination of Bach's work as a church musician was reached in his settings of the Passion according to St. John and St. Matthew. These two works, essentially similar in structure, are the crowning examples of the north German tradition of Gospel Passion settings in oratorio style."[231]

Although Bach encountered subsequent conflicts with his superiors, his discipline and handling of the choral scholars during practices and performances were never questioned. This fact is in contrast to his predecessors, who were admonished for their lack of control and loose discipline. Bach utilized a strict schedule of fines designed to discourage students from disturbing performances. Students could be fined for a noticeable mistake and heavily penalized for intentional and mischievous errors. The collected money was used to buy music and maintain instruments. In the twenty-seven years Bach served in Leipzig, he supervised and directed "some 1,500 performances of cantatas, passions, oratorios, and similar works to captive audience of more than two thousand each time."[232] He further strengthened the worship music in the church by reorganizing the organists. He moved Johann Gottlieb Görner from St. Paul's to St. Thomas's and appointed two of his students, Carl Gotthelf Gerlach and Johann Schneider, at New Church and St. Nicholas. So well did Bach place these players that all three of them remained at their posts for the rest of their careers.[233]

Bach's two main conflicts with his superiors during these early days in Leipzig both concerned the prerogatives of his office. In the first conflict, the university initiated new services at the university chapel and reduced the cantor's role and payment for the old services, which were part of his duties. The fact that the other organist involved in the controversy was Görner, Bach's later appointee to St. Thomas, indicates that the situation was not personal and involved instead the authority and rights of Bach's office. The second conflict involved the responsibility to choose the hymns for the services. One of the ministers decided to start choosing hymns that were not from an approved list, did not correlate to the assigned hymns of the day, and omitted the creed. Bach's stance on this point referred to the prerogatives of his office in the defense of the music and worship of the church.

In 1727 Bach took over the direction of the *Collegium Musicum,* an orchestra made up almost entirely of university students who played weekly concerts at Zimmermann's Coffeehouse. In the winter, these concerts took place in town, and in the summer they occurred outside the city gates in Zimmermann's Garden. Admission was

free, and patrons would gather to hear the music, converse, smoke, and drink coffee and beer. The members of
the ensemble were flexible, and their numbers changed
regularly with up to forty players participating. Visiting
players were also allowed to sit in and play. Bach was
responsible for providing music and rehearsals for the
weekly concerts. Since this was not a school activity, Bach
was not able to utilize students to help copy parts—a task
that fell to his wife and children.[234]

Bach expressed some of his frustrations from this period in a letter he wrote to his schoolmate from Ohrdruf
and Lüneburg, Georg Erdmann. He said of Leipzig, "Here,
by God's will I am still in service."[235] His concerns included the fact that the post was "by no means so lucrative as it was described to me," he had "failed to obtain
many of the fees pertaining to the office," Leipzig was an
expensive place to live, and "the authorities are odd and
little interested in music, so that I must live amid almost
continual vexation, envy, and persecution."[236] Bach also
witnessed the beginnings of Enlightenment influences
that sought to weaken the music in the school in favor of
other studies by admitting students who were not competent in music—one of the stated requirements for admit-
tance. This slide toward secular principles had a short
reprieve in the next few years, but then the fight was renewed in earnest.

INTERLUDE
CHURCH MUSIC

*And Johann Sebastian Bach expressed his faith
and his dedication to God's glory, as well as his
mastery of musical concepts, in patterns of sound
and harmony.*[237]

BACH'S FIRST FEW YEARS in Leipzig were marked
by a prodigious outpouring of music for the
service of the church. In a period of about thirty months,
Bach wrote almost 150 church cantatas. At the very least,
the *St. John* and *St. Matthew Passions* were products of
his first four years. Other music written during these years
included motets, choral movements from the Mass, and
the Easter Oratorio.

The texts of the cantatas were closely associated with
the hymn of the day, the Gospel of the day, the exposition
of the Gospel in the sermon, and the confession of faith in
Luther's creedal hymn.[238] The texts themselves consisted
of Bible passages, stanzas from hymns, and religious poetry, "the whole illustrating some Scripture theme."[239]

Bach's production schedule for his weekly writing followed a regular pattern:

1. Select or have selected (by clergy) the text (also arrange texts—approximately six per cantata booklet—and prepare about twelve such booklets per year for publication).
2. Compose choruses, arias, recitatives, and chorales—generally in that order (beginning Monday, if not before); prepare the music paper and score, and write the more elaborate movements first, to allow enough time for copying and rehearsing.
3. Organize and supervise the copying effort to make performance parts (assemble the copyists around tables in the cantor's office and the library).
4. Review the performance materials (proofread, correct, enter articulation and other performance markings).
5. Conduct rehearsals (generally no more than one complete read-through on Saturday).[240]

Bach wrote the music of the cantatas to reflect the various texts and to provide a musical illustration of the theological content of the words. These were intended as musical sermons to edify the congregation and to bring glory to God through the proclamation of truth. The text generally opens with a passage from the prescribed Gospel lesson as a point for departure and is sung by the full choir. Explanations of the passage in the form of other Scripture references, doctrinal statements, or elements of the original text are conveyed through recitatives (short, declamatory sections) and arias (lyrical movements for solo or duet). The "considerations of the consequences to be drawn from the lesson and the admonition to conduct a true Christian life" are also expressed through recitatives and arias.[241] The cantata concludes with the use of a hymn stanza, which acts as a corporate prayer with the congregation joining in with the singing.[242]

The Passions follow a long tradition of chanting or singing the words of Scripture pertaining to the Crucifixion, which goes back to the early church. These were essentially dramatic works with soloists taking the spoken parts of the various characters but singing only the words of Scripture itself. Bach included chorales and choral numbers that comment upon the narrative and provide opportunity for reflection and prayer. Bach was skillful at interweaving various musical and theological concepts, which not only told the Passion story but made application to his listeners in such a manner that involved them in the immediacy of the story. The application of the work of the Cross to the individual and corporate lives of the congregation made these works powerful in their own day as well as timeless in their effectiveness.

The Passions last several hours and end with Christ still in the grave—appropriate for a Good Friday service. Bach had the liturgical opportunity to reflect upon the death and sacrifice of Christ but then to rejoice in the Resurrection through the occasion of Easter music, such as the Easter Oratorio.

Bach also wrote various motets and movements from the Mass. In his liturgical reforms, Martin Luther maintained many of the elements from the Catholic Mass and daily liturgy such as the *Kyrie, Gloria,* and *Magnificat.* Luther also retained the singing of various texts in Latin as part of the church services.[243]

Bach wrote a wealth of music for the church in a very short period of time. Unfortunately, the vast majority of it has been neglected. As Calvin Stapert explains, "The reason Bach's cantatas, in the eyes of posterity, moved from the center to the periphery is the post-Enlightenment preference for generic religious feeling over an explicit Christian message. Bach's cantatas do not fit that bill; they are nothing if not explicitly Christian. . . . The emphasis in the canonical Bach [that which is most frequently performed and discussed] is on the instrumental music. The vocal music, of course, is not totally ignored, but the post-Enlightenment mind accepts it only after mentally divorcing the music from the explicitly Christian content of its texts."[244]

Bach still has much to teach the church, not only about music, but about the appropriate use of artistic gifts in service to the glory of God and for the instruction of the believer.

CONFLICT AND RESOLVE
1730s

*What becomes evident here is that in the 1730s,
Bach's composing desk became the work site for a
creative mind more exploring, self-critical, and far-
ranging than ever before. His continuing output of
new works was complemented by an intensified
review of the extant repertoire, a persistent
process of improving smaller and larger details,
and a systematically cultivated campaign of
parodying and arranging—with the goal not of
exploiting or multiplying extant works but rather
of opening new horizons for them.*[245]

ITH ENLIGHTENMENT IDEALS BEGINNING to affect his daily job, Bach remained frus-
trated at the council's, at best, apparent lack of regard for
what was needed to produce the caliber of music he had
thus attained, or, at worst, their desire to follow other
principles that would intentionally minimize Bach's work.
The opportunity for some change occurred when the rector, Johann Heinrich Ernesti, died on October 16, 1729.
At age seventy-seven, he had been the headmaster since

1684. With that vacancy, the council had an opportunity to influence the direction of the St. Thomas School.[246]

As an older man, Rector Ernesti was resistant to any change and had let the school deteriorate. "Standards of conduct, discipline, and instruction had declined, and the physical condition of the buildings left much to be desired. Dormitories were overcrowded and insanitary, with boys sometimes having to share a bed, and as many as three different classes at a time were held in one schoolroom."[247] The appointment of Johann Mattias Gesner in June 1730 was greeted with great hope for a promising new beginning. One city councillor stated that with this appointment he "wished that it would be better than with the cantor."[248]

Gesner knew Bach from their time together in Weimar, and he shared the same beliefs as Bach regarding the importance of music in both the school and the church. Bach now had an ally who not only supported him but also admired him and his abilities.[249] In 1738 Gesner wrote an illustration of Bach playing and conducting and described him as

not only . . . singing with one voice and playing his own parts, but watching over everything and bringing back to the rhythm and the beat, out of thirty or even forty musicians, the one with a nod, another by tapping with his foot, the third with a warning finger, giving the right note to one from the top of his voice, to another from the bottom, and to a third from the middle of it—all alone, in the midst of the greatest din made by all the participants, and, although he is executing the most difficult parts himself, noticing at once whenever and wherever a mistake occurs, holding everyone together, taking precautions everywhere, and repairing any unsteadiness, full of rhythm in every part of his body—this one man taking in all these harmonies with his keen ear and emitting with his voice alone the tone of all the voices.[250]

The new start promised with the appointment of Gesner began to take shape as he helped to restore the relationship between Bach and the council and started an extensive renovation and enlargement of the St. Thomas School beginning in the spring of 1731. Part of the renovation included the addition of two stories to the facility. Bach and his family were moved off campus during the fourteen months of construction.[251]

The school was rededicated in an official ceremony on June 5, 1732. For the occasion, Bach composed the cantata "Happy day, longed-for-hours," for which the text was printed in a decorative edition of one hundred copies and in five hundred regular copies.[252]

On February 1, 1733, the elector of Saxony, Friedrich August I (King August II of Poland), died, and an official period of mourning was declared for the next five months with no new church music. Bach used this time off to write a large-scale choral *Kyrie* and *Gloria,* two movements common to both the Lutheran liturgy and Catholic Mass. Bach's desire was to present the music to the new elector, Friedrich August II (King August III), in hopes of being honored with a court title. Bach was able to present the works directly to the court when he traveled to Dresden in July 1733 to be at the installation of his oldest son,

Wilhelm Friedemann Bach, as organist at St. Sophia's Church in Dresden.[253]

Bach wrote several more pieces for the elector and his family, culminating in a work in honor of the elector's accession to the throne. This piece was performed in Leipzig with August II in attendance. At 9:00 p.m. a procession of six hundred students carrying torches made their way to the marketplace, where the cantata was sung with much fanfare. In 1736 August II at last granted Bach's request and conferred upon Bach the title of "Composer to the Royal Court Capelle" because of his "humble entreaty and because of his ability."[254] A Dresden newspaper reported:

> The famous capellmeister to the Prince of Saxe-Weissenfels and Director Musices at Leipzig, Mr. Johann Sebastian Bach, made himself heard from 2 to 4 o'clock on the new organ in the church of Our Lady, in the presence of . . . many persons of rank, also a large attendance of other persons and artists, with particular admiration, wherefore also His Royal Majesty most graciously named the same, because of his great ability in composing, to be His Majesty's Composer.[255]

At the time of this honor, Bach must surely have wished for greater respect from the city council because of continued conflict. Rector Gesner had been able to institute mild organizational reforms and to uphold the place of music in the curriculum. He reminded the council that "our ancestors intended the school to be a seminary of music whereby the singing in all our churches might be provided."[256] Unfortunately for Bach and for the St. Thomas School, Gesner resigned in 1734 because of a clause in his contract that prevented him from holding any university posts in addition to his teaching at St. Thomas. The council replaced Gesner in 1734 with Johann August Ernesti (1707–81), whose desire was to transform the school "into a progressive academy embodying Enlightenment principles."[257]

Ernesti, who was no direct relation to the former St. Thomas rector, "challenged basic assumptions of the old curriculum and in particular the place of music as the handmaid to theology."[258] As Bach biographer Russell Miles explained, Ernesti had "little regard and less tolerance for church music," and he "began a long-range program of attrition aimed at cutting extra choir activities to the bone, and greatly curtailing the rehearsal hours for the regular church services. He usurped Bach's prerogative of choir administrator, accused him of neglecting academic duties, and even, at times, impugned his integrity."[259] The main issue for Bach was the ability to execute the worship music in such a manner as to bring God glory. The reduction of his rehearsals and the usurping of his authority challenged the ability to prepare and adequately equip students for the task of leading in worship.

"The position of music in the school was under constant threat from Enlightenment principles, which saw value only in the 'relevant,' up-to-date subjects."[260] Because of this, students were allowed to enroll in St. Thomas School who did not have the background, inclination, or ability to be a part of the core music program of the school. Conflict with Ernesti specifically exploded over the right to appoint student leaders, or prefects, over the choirs. This particular conflict lasted several years and even disrupted church services on occasion. Through it all, Bach's aim was the protection of the students under his care and the guarding of the church's worship.

Despite the conflicts, Bach continued to write and perform new works. During Christmas of 1734, Bach presented his Christmas Oratorio in six parts according to the following schedule:

Part One—Christmas Day;
Part Two—The Second Day of Christmas;
Part Three—The Third Day of Christmas;
Part Four—New Year's Day—The Feast Day of
   the Circumcision;
Part Five—The Sunday after New Year's Day;
Part Six—The Feast Day of Epiphany.[261]

Bach significantly utilized the chorale melody known as the Passion chorale ("O Sacred Head Now Wounded") at the beginning and end of the Christmas Oratorio. Bach was thus able to musically and theologically link the birth of Christ with the redemptive purpose of the Incarnation through a reminder of Christ's death.

In 1735 Bach began the process of writing the genealogy of his family and collecting music by his kin in what became known as the Old-Bach Archive. He also started spending more time reviewing his previous compositions and making changes and amendments. It was around this time that he prepared the fair copy of the *St. Matthew Passion,* meticulously drawing the lines with a straight-edge and writing the words from Scripture in red ink. The 1730s witnessed the publication of Bach's *Clavier-Übung* series (literally "keyboard practice") in four parts from 1731 to 1741—a "systematic and complete survey of the art of keyboard music as seen from Bach's perspective."[262] Bach presented almost a catalog of compositional techniques and forms that set new performance standards.

The third volume of the *Clavier-Übung* is a series of chorale preludes on hymn tunes from the Lutheran catechism and the *Kyrie* and *Gloria* from the Mass. Bach used the music in this volume to explore the doctrine of the Trinity as articulated in the catechism. "In symbolic recognition of the dogma of the Trinity, Bach writes for conclusion a triple fugue with a key signature of three flats; each of the three sections of the fugue has its own subject, with increasing rhythmic animation, and the first subject is combined contrapuntally with each of the other two."[263]

In October 1737 Johann Elias Bach joined the household as a secretary and a tutor to Bach's young children. Elias was a cousin of Bach's, and he stayed with the family for five years, during which time he studied theology at the university and maintained Bach's correspondence. When he left in October 1742, he took a teaching position, but the following year he took a position as a cantor.[264]

The late 1730s brought a direct attack on Bach through a series of articles against him and the principles and beliefs to which he adhered. These critiques essentially accused Bach of being old-fashioned by obscuring natural ideas with an excess of art. Coming from an Enlightenment perspective that prized individuality and sensual experience over craftsmanship and historical continuity, the criticism was groundless from a biblical perspective. However, the sharp comments caused Bach to retreat and reassess his art as he approached the final decade of his life.

DOMESTIC LIFE IN LEIPZIG

*Bach seems to have been warm-hearted,
generous, and hospitable in his own home. A
man who enjoyed a pipe, who liked his wine and
beer, and who fathered twenty children cannot
have been indifferent to sensual pleasures, and
during the period of his greatest celebrity in
Leipzig he was always ready to receive the many
visitors who sought him out.[265]*

WHEN BACH AND ANNA MAGDALENA moved to
Leipzig in 1723, their household included
Maria Barbara's four surviving children (Catharina
Dorothea, Wilhelm Friedemann, Carl Philipp Emanuel,
and Johann Gottfried Bernhard) and Magdalena's newborn
daughter, Christiana Sophia Henrietta. Magdalena gave
birth to thirteen children over a period of nineteen years in
Leipzig; only six survived to adulthood. Between the years
of 1723 and 1733, Magdalena bore ten children and lost
seven of them. The infant mortality rate decreased sharply
after the renovations were completed to the St. Thomas
School, raising speculation that the cantor's rebuilt apartment offered better hygienic conditions for infants.

When the family moved back into their quarters in April 1732, they gained two floors of space and several new rooms. The front door could be answered by a pull mechanism that opened the door from the second-floor living room, which overlooked the square. The ground floor contained two rooms—only one heated. Bach's office, the kitchen, main living room, and the master bedroom were all on the second floor. All of the bedrooms were unheated. The total space in the apartment amounted to about 802 square feet. Although big by the standards of the day, the house surely felt crowded with the presence of all the children, other family members who lived with them, and the numerous visitors who sought out Bach for fellowship or professional reasons.[266]

From all accounts, Bach doted on his wife. As a musician, she understood her husband's work, and from the number of manuscripts copied by her own hand, it is obvious that she knew his music thoroughly. They shared a love of music and the joy and sorrow that bearing and losing children can bring. Extant letters show Bach's kindness and joy in obtaining gifts for her. She continued to sing in Cöthen as a soloist after her marriage to Bach. However, the only documented evidence of her performing after their move to Leipzig were trips back to Cothen to present music for Prince Leopold.

After his sons established their own careers (often with his letters of recommendation), Bach followed the professional activities of his sons and visited his two eldest as often as he could. Friedemann attended the University of Leipzig and then accepted an organist position in Dresden and later Halle. Carl Philipp Emanuel studied law and then accepted a musical position at the court of Frederick the Great at Potsdam.[267] Bach did not live long enough to see the success of his younger sons, Johann Christoph Friedrich and Johann Christian.

Johann Gottfried Bernhard, the youngest child of Maria Barbara, brought grief to his father. An apparently dissolute young man who lacked self-control, he squandered two job opportunities that Bach secured for him as organist in Mühlhausen and Sangerhausen. He ran up debts and then skipped town on both occasions. For a long time his father did not even know where he was. At the time of his death at the age of twenty-four, he was enrolled as a law student at the University in Jena, suggesting that he perhaps had settled down.

Bach taught a large number of students throughout his career. The amount of time he devoted to writing pieces for the purpose of instruction, to individually working with students, and to ensuring that his students were well placed with jobs is unparalleled in the history of art music composers. What joy he must have had when his daughter Elisabeth Juliana Friederica (affectionately known as Lieschen) married Johann Christoph Altnickol, one of his best students.[268] "If we consider the great number of pupils who were taught by Johann Sebastian Bach after his time in Weimar, many of whom themselves became important musicians and teachers, it is not surprising that large parts of Bach's piano and organ works were very widely distributed throughout the 18th century."[269]

By all accounts his gregarious personality endeared him to students and visitors alike. As one student said, "His sober temperament largely drew him to industrious, serious and deep music, but when it seemed necessary he could also think in a more light-hearted and jocular manner, especially in games."[270] Carl Philipp Emanuel referred to his father's house as a pigeon house "with all the coming and going" of "good people."[271] "Association with him was pleasant for everyone, and often very edifying."[272]

In addition to his teaching schedule, composing projects, and steady stream of private pupils, Bach also engaged in other enterprises. Bach published his own music, rented instruments and music, acted as a sales agent for other publishers and instrument makers, inspected organs in various cities, designed improvements for existing instruments, and performed with the *Collegium Musicum* and privately.[273]

Despite the struggles and annoyances of his time in Leipzig, Bach led a rich and varied life with numerous opportunities of his own making. What fun he must have had preparing music parts with his family and performing music with his sons. The fact that Bach stayed in Leipzig the rest of his life and did not actively seek another appointment (his letter to his friend Georg Erdmann in 1730 notwithstanding) indicates that he must have felt a sense of vocation in the work he accomplished there. He was in a unique position to fulfill his calling toward well-regulated church music with an opportunity to stand in the gap to preserve and protect, defend, and develop the music and worship of the church. As he wrote about his position in Leipzig, he said, "Here, by God's will I am still in service." And there he continued to faithfully serve.

NEW HEIGHTS
1740s

The tendency of Bach in his later years [was] to concern himself with the greatest intricacies of his art. As he grew older, he reduced what he said more and more to its essentials. Less than ever concerned with worldly success, he sought perfection increasingly in the utmost consistency of logic and construction.[274]

IN LATE MARCH 1739 the city council sent a clerk to Bach to tell him "that the music he intends to perform on the coming Good Friday is to be omitted until regular permission for the same is received."[275] With the stroke of a pen and no explanation, Bach's music was canceled ten days before the service. That Bach was planning a performance of the *St. John Passion* seems evident from a revision of the piece started in the late 1730s that breaks off suddenly in the middle of a movement.[276]

Although Bach performed Passion music on subsequent Good Fridays, the sudden demand of the council must have come as a shock and a severe disappointment. Although in and of itself this appears to be a minor incident, it does foreshadow a shift in Bach's work habits during the decade of the 1740s. There is no question that he fulfilled his duties and executed them admirably, but the focus of his work changed. There is evidence that Bach wrote only one portion of a new church cantata during this period.[277] Although there was a radical shift in his compositional activities, he did already have a library filled with around three hundred cantatas to choose from. And with changing students and instrumentalists, the works remained new to the performers and fresh to the congregation, who heard the works only every five years.

Bach turned his focus to what has been termed the *Summa,* or summation, works—compositions of such beauty, erudition, achievement, and comprehensiveness that they approach musical perfection and rival any intellectual accomplishment in the history of man. The philosophical and theological bases for these works correspond to the aims and ideals of the Society of Musical Science (Mizler's society), which Bach joined in 1747.

Lorenz Christoph Mizler studied theology at the University of Leipzig from 1731 to 1734 and also studied music with Bach. Most likely he played flute and violin under Bach in the *Collegium Musicum* as well. As someone knowledgeable in a variety of subject areas, a true polymath, Mizler sought understanding and wisdom that connected these areas, with "one of his keenest interests being to find a firm mathematical and philosophical basis for musical science."[278] Mizler's master's thesis in 1734 was titled *Quod musica ars sit pars eruditionis philosophicae* (On whether the art of music is part of philosophic wisdom).[279]

In 1738 Mizler founded the Society of Musical Sciences, a corresponding society that "aimed at fostering contacts among the regular members by mailing twice a year, at around Easter and St. Michael's Day, a circular containing musical news, essays, and practical and theoretical works contributed or selected by the membership."[280] Mizler persuaded Bach to join in 1747 as the fourteenth member. Membership required the submission of a test piece and a portrait, the familiar pose of Bach actually holding his test composition. The test piece was a six-voice canon and a set of canonic variations of the Christmas Chorale, "From Heaven Above to Earth I Come," in which "the strict imitations are woven around the chorale tune so intricately, yet so deftly, as to have reduced great composers of succeeding generations to incredulity. . . . A technical analysis takes the mind to giddy heights, yet the music speaks directly to the heart of the untutored listener."[281] A canon is essentially a "round" in which the melody enters at different times on top of itself.

Bach viewed the very basic elements of music "as constituting a religious reality, that the more perfectly the task of composition (and, indeed, performance) is realized, the more God is immanent in music."[282] The parallels between the "harmony of music and that of creation" built upon the medieval theocentric understanding of the universe in which everything finds its intersection point in the nature and character of God.[283] As Bach's obituary stated, "If ever a musician employed the most hidden secrets of harmony with the most skilled artistry, it was certainly our Bach," and in so doing, he expanded the very idea of music by utilizing godly wisdom and discernment over all its elements on a multiplicity of levels.[284]

Since 1740, Carl Philipp Emanuel had held the position of harpsichordist to Frederick the Great. Frederick was curious to hear Sebastian Bach play, since he had heard so much about him. He hinted to Bach's son that he would like to meet his father and finally started asking directly "why his father did not come."[285] Bach arrived in Potsdam in May 1747 with his son Friedemann. Carl Philipp Emanuel married in 1744, and his first son, Johann August, was born in December 1745. Because of hostilities between Prussia and Saxony, Bach had been unable to meet his daughter-in-law or his first grandchild until this trip.[286]

Frederick the Great ordinarily had chamber music played from 7:00 to 9:00 p.m. daily. From reports given by Bach's sons, Johann Nikolaus Forkel told of the encounter in his 1802 biography of Bach:

At this time the King used to have every evening a private concert in which he himself generally performed some concertos on the flute. One evening [May 7, 1747], just as he was getting his flute ready and his musicians were arrived, an officer brought him the written list of the strangers who had arrived. With his flute in his hand, he ran over the list, but immediately turned to the assembled musicians and said, with a kind of agitation: "Gentlemen, old Bach is come." The flute was now laid aside, and old Bach, who had alighted at his son's lodgings, was immediately summoned to the Palace. . . .

[T]he King gave up his concert for this evening and invited Bach, then already called the Old Bach, to try his fortepianos . . . which stood in several rooms of the

Palace. The musicians went with him from room to room, and Bach was invited everywhere to try them and to play unpremeditated compositions. After he had gone on for some time, he asked the King to give him a subject for a fugue in order to execute it immediately without preparation. The King admired the learned manner in which his subject was thus executed.[287]

The king pushed Bach to play the theme to its limits, including a fugue in six parts. Instead, Bach chose another theme and executed that one in a six-voice texture. Bach further told the king that he would execute the royal theme in six voices on paper once he returned home. The following day the king took Bach to all of the organs in Potsdam in order to hear Bach perform on them.

By July 1747 Bach had completed a large multipart composition built around the king's musical theme, which Bach dedicated to Frederick and published as the *Musical Offering.* "In some ways, the work conceals a musical self-portrait: of a composer in his capacity as keyboard genius and master of fugue, capellmeister and chamber musician, contrapuntalist and musical scholar."[288]

In 1733 Bach wrote *Kyrie* and *Gloria* movements from the Mass on a grand scale for the new elector Augustus II. During the late 1740s Bach completed the rest of the movements for the Mass in B Minor: *Credo, Sanctus,* and *Agnus Dei.* There is a tendency to question Bach's motives as a Protestant in setting the text of the Mass; however, Martin Luther "was by no means inclined to break with all the forms and usages of the mother Church. He had no quarrel with those features of her rites which did not embody the doctrines which he disavowed, and most heartily did he recognize the beauty and edifying power of Catholic music."[289] Regarding the use of Latin, Luther himself was in favor of retaining Latin in communities in which it was understood. In addition, "the forms of the Latin texts that Bach employed reflect Lutheran rather than Catholic usage, and the division of the Mass into four, rather than the traditional five Catholic sections, underscores its Lutheran origins."[290]

Bach brought his rhetorical abilities to full bear in the symbolic elements with which he conveyed the truth of the text and the gospel. Bach divided the *Credo,* or Nicene Creed, into nine sections of music with the phrases "and was crucified also for us under Pontius Pilate. He suffered and was buried," as the fifth of the nine sections. As such, the "Crucifixus" appears at the center of the profession of faith. The center of the creed, musically and theologically, is the doctrine of propitiation and the sacrifice of Christ.

The *Sanctus,* or "Holy, Holy, Holy," comes from the passage in Isaiah 6:1–3, in which the prophet sees the Lord God surrounded by angels with six wings who cry "Holy!" Bach set this movement with six voice parts. In addition:

Bach's *Sanctus* abounds in sixes, threes and twos, not only illustrating the Isaiah 6 passage but also symbolizing the traditional interpretation of the Sanctus as a Trinitarian hymn in which each "Sanctus" is addressed to each of the three Persons of the Trinity in turn. The movement is the only six-part writing in his ecclesiastical choral works, and, in addition to timpani and continuo, calls for an orchestra made up of three trumpets, three oboes, and three strings. Further, it makes emphatic use of triplets, especially in the opening bars; it often calls for three vocal parts to be contrasted against the full six-part texture; and on two occasions—both for the duration of three bars—the three highest voices and the three lowest voices call back and forth to each other, imitating the Seraphim of Isaiah's vision.[291]

Bach never heard a complete performance of the Mass in B Minor because the piece was on too grand a scale to be part of a worship service, and a secular performance in a concert setting would have been deemed inappropriate. The Mass as composed is more than anything a devout expression of personal faith that is the height of artistry and a capstone of Bach's music for the church. It is a compendium of musical styles, vocal techniques, and compositions that incorporates the best from the history of church music with the creativity of Bach's more recent musical pinnacle. "So vast is it in scale, so majestic in its movement, so elemental in the grandeur of its climaxes, that it may well be taken as the loftiest expression in tones of the prophetic faith of Christendom."[292]

The Art of Fugue was the product of a decade-long fascination with exploring every possibility and element of writing for multiple voices in imitative fashion. Musicians for 250 years "have been awed by the incredible technique and ingenuity with which Bach, in *The Art of the Fugue,* summarized everything known about counterpoint and then added the full measure of his own mighty genius, creating a score that in its majesty and poetry stands unique."[293] Called "one of the loftiest accomplishments of the human mind,"[294] Bach explored and codified the ideas of counterpoint and fugue such that "never has a fugue been made by any composer which could be compared with one of his. He who is not acquainted with Bach's fugues cannot even form an idea of what a true fugue is and ought to be."[295]

The 1740s offered Bach the opportunity to refine, polish, and perfect his craft to hitherto unknown potentials. His heights of achievement were matched only by the depth of theological understanding and purpose that pervaded all aspects of his work. The aims of the Mizler society in harmonizing seemingly disparate fields of knowledge found their correspondence in the works and art of Bach. He had reached the point of rhetoric, or true wisdom, in the application and apologetics of his craft.

A DISHONORED PROPHET AND REVIVAL

*He enjoyed some reputation in Protestant
Germany as an organ virtuoso and writer of
learned contrapuntal works, but there were at
least a half-dozen contemporary composers who
were more widely known in Europe. He regarded
himself as a conscientious craftsman doing a job
to the best of his ability for the satisfaction of his
superiors, for the pleasure and edification of his
fellowmen, and to the glory of God.[296]*

IN LATE SPRING 1749, Bach apparently encountered serious health problems. The exact nature
of his infirmity and the extent of the illness are not
known. However, what is known is that the city council
heard a trial performance of Bach's replacement in antici-
pation of "the eventual occasion of the decease of Mr.
Bach."[297] The Saxon prime minister sent the composer of
his *capelle,* Gottlob Harrer, to Leipzig with a letter of recommendation and the full assurance that this premature
audition would meet with approbation and produce a cer-
tificate ensuring Harrer the position.

On June 8, 1749, Harrer presented a trial performance at the Three Swans concert hall for the position of cantor at St. Thomas School, "in case . . . Mr. Sebastian Bach should die." All of the conditions surrounding this audition were out of the ordinary. Other than the obvious fact that Bach was not yet dead, the cantata performance took place outside of the church and on a weekday because Bach was still in charge of the church music program. It is entirely possible that the first choir from St. Thomas School and the best instrumentalists were not utilized because of the unorthodox manner of this trial.

Bach was back to church by June 19, where he received Communion and then set about to dismiss any thoughts of his death or replacement. In August he presented for the city council election service one of his most ambitious cantatas, which included a part for an organ solo—no doubt an opportunity to display his considerable ability in the face of any detractors. In the late summer or fall, Bach re-presented his secular cantata "The Contest Between Pheobus and Pan" with the *Collegium Musicum.* This work pits the forces of high art and good artistic judgment against those of low art and poor judgment—a virtual commentary of the events of the preceding months. Bach also enabled his sons Friedemann and Carl Philipp Emanuel to present works at St. Thomas's and St. Nicholas's on prominent feast days, thus elevating their names as potential successors.

In late March 1750 Bach submitted to a surgical procedure on his eyes by a visiting doctor from England. Carl Philipp Emanuel and a former student wrote Bach's official obituary, in which they stated:

His naturally somewhat weak eye sight, further weakened by his unheard-of-zeal in studying, which made him, particularly in his youth, sit at work the whole night through, led, in his last years, to an eye disease. He wished to rid himself of this by an operation, partly out of a desire to be of further service to God and his neighbor with his other spiritual and bodily powers, which were still very vigorous, and partly on the advice of some of his friends, who placed great confidence in an oculist who had recently arrived in Leipzig. But the operation, although it had to be repeated, turned out badly. Not only could he no longer use his eyes, but his whole system, which was otherwise thoroughly healthy, was completely overthrown by the operation and by the addition of harmful medicaments and other things.[298]

Bach remained ill, and probably blind, for the next several months. By May 1750 Bach accepted a new boarding student into his home. Presumably he was at least stabilized if not getting better.

Ten days before his death his eyes suddenly seemed better, so that one morning he could see quite well again and could also again endure the light. But a few hours later he suffered a stroke; and this was followed by a raging fever, as a victim of which, despite every possible care given him by two of the most skillful physicians of Leipzig, on July 28, 1750, a little after a quarter past eight in the evening, in the sixty-sixth year of his life, he quietly and peacefully, by the merit of his Redeemer, departed life.[299]

After the stroke on July 20, Bach must have recognized that his end was near. Two days later, the archdeacon at St. Thomas's Church, Bach's "longtime father confessor," visited his sickbed and administered the sacrament. From his deathbed, Bach dictated to his son-in-law Altnickol the music of a chorale whose words were "Before Your Throne I Now Appear"—a final testimony of his faith in God and his hope of eternal life.[300]

One of the last works on which Bach worked with his own hand was a set of instrumental parts to complement the vocal parts of a double choir work composed by his uncle, Johann Christoph. This score was most likely prepared as his own funereal piece with a traditional prayer text that looks forward to life after death:

> Dear Lord God, wake us up,
> So that we are prepared when Thy Son comes,
> To receive him with joy
> And to serve Thee with a pure heart,
> By the same, Thy dear son,
> Jesus Christ. Amen.[301]

Of all the music that he himself wrote, it is interesting that Bach chose the work of another family member to be sung at his memorial service.

The following announcement was read during the Friday afternoon prayer service on July 31, 1750:

> Peacefully and blissfully departed in God the Esteemed and Highly Respected Mr. Johann Sebastian Bach, Court Composer to His Royal Majesty in Poland and Serene

Electoral Highness in Saxony, as well as Capellmeister to the Prince of Anhalt-Cöthen and Cantor in the St. Thomas School, at the Square of St. Thomas's his dead body was this day in accordance with Christian usage committed to the earth.[302]

Bach was buried in St. John's cemetery, with no gravestone or marker to signify the place where he was laid.

Bach was survived by Anna Magdalena and nine children, four of whom were minors and one, Gottfried Heinrich, who needed perpetual care. Gottfried Heinrich went to live with his sister Elisabeth and her husband, Altnickol, in Naumburg until his death in 1763. Altnickol died in 1759, but Carl Philipp Emanuel sent a regular allowance to his widow. Carl Philipp Emanuel also took in his younger half brother Johann Christian and taught him until 1754 when he left for Italy. Apparently none of the family were able or felt obligated to assist Anna Magdalena, who was left with an unmarried stepdaughter and two younger daughters (ages thirteen and eight). She existed on charity at an almshouse, where she died in February 1760 and was then buried in a pauper's grave.[303]

In the absence of a will, Bach's wife received one-third of his estate, with the remaining portion divided among his children.[304] None of Bach's musical scores or manuscripts are listed in an otherwise-detailed inventory of his belongings, indicating that Bach must have divided his musical estate before his death between his wife and sons. Anna Magdalena gave her cantata parts to the St. Thomas School in exchange for six months' residency. Those works remained safe over the years. The dissemination of the cantata scores suggests that each of the yearly cycles was shared by two heirs. The music given to Anna Magdalena and Carl Philipp Emanuel remains the most complete scores still in existence.

The music given to sons Johann Christoph Friedrich, Wilhelm Friedemann, and Johann Christian was, for the most part, lost.[305] Bach's music was already out of favor at the time of his death, with the taste of the day chasing after the sensual and simple melodies of the Enlightenment composers. At least two of the sons sold, gave away, and auctioned their copies of music for the money—Friedemann to subsidize his dissolute lifestyle; and Johann Christian to finance his trip to Italy, where he converted to Catholicism. As Carl Philipp Emanuel indicated in a penned note next to Johann Christian's name in the Bach genealogy, "between ourselves, he did things differently from honest Veit."[306] "Bach's sons, with the possible exception of Johann Christian (who is rumored to have referred to Johann Sebastian as "the old wig"), held his father's work in high esteem, but Carl Philipp Emanuel was the only one among them who actively worked to increase Johann Sebastian's fame and make his works more generally known."[307]

The pervading change in the theological climate and, by extension, the musical culture caused a great abandoning of Bach's works—especially his vocal works. The prevailing ideology of the times could not rectify itself to the pointed and direct theological teachings inherent in Bach's works for the church. His keyboard works, however, were distributed and copied through the efforts of his numerous students as they themselves used his music to teach others. In the meantime, years of disuse and careless oversight of manuscripts resulted in the loss of countless works by Bach.

Traces of comments and stories from Mozart, Beethoven, and others indicate that Bach was not completely forgotten, but he was sorely neglected and marginalized. As a young man, Felix Mendelssohn, composer and performer and himself a Lutheran, explored the works of "old Sebastian" and made it his life's work to restore Bach to his rightful place of honor. With the revival of the *St. Matthew Passion* in 1829 under the direction of the twenty-year-old Mendelssohn, the formation of the German Bach Society in the 1840s, and the publication of the complete works of Bach (forty-six volumes from 1850 to 1900), the music of Bach began to receive increased notice and awareness.

Bach fulfilled a unique position as one who manifested multiple paradoxes in his work. Bach composed music for immediate occasions but in a manner that made them timeless; Bach composed music of sublime erudition and wisdom that bewildered the experts but in a manner that still made it accessible for the common person; Bach composed music that defied the tastes of the day but in a manner that far outlived the transient works. Bach composed for God's glory and not his own, and because of that, God continues to be glorified through Bach's music, and Bach himself is honored as well.

Part 2

The Character of Johann Sebastian Bach

There's nothing remarkable about it. All one has to do is hit the right keys at the right time and the instrument plays itself.

—Johann Sebastian Bach

ACCESSIBLE YET PROFOUND

*It is not really surprising that the compositional
mastery of Bach's music should inspire the artist,
that its philological and other problems should
fascinate the scholar, or that its technical
challenges should be taken up by the performer.
What is astonishing, and in the end inexplicable,
is that music which makes so few concessions
to the listener should enjoy an immense
popular following.[1]*

ONE OF THE GREATEST struggles in anyone's calling is the tension between being accessible
yet profound. Accessibility is necessary in order to be understood, to effect change, to communicate knowledge
and wisdom. Profundity is necessary in order to be undi-
luted and unnecessarily simple, to offer depths and layers
of meaning, to develop and mature people. The friction
exists in meeting people where they are but then not
leaving them there. Bach's answer to that question was
to write music people could readily understand, but he
did so in such a way that music scholars still struggle to
plumb its depths.

The key to much of Bach's work was his use of well-known chorales. During the Reformation, Martin Luther created a thunderous liturgical reform with the introduction of vernacular hymns for the purpose of engaging the congregation in song and theological training. Many of the great truths of the gospel were set to music to be more readily absorbed by the people. In 1524, the leaders of the Reformation published four collections of these chorale tunes and texts, with others following at frequent intervals.[2] These chorales were specific to the sermons of each Sunday "so that eventually every Sunday, festival and special celebration had its own particular hymnody. By the eighteenth century these 'hymns of the day' had grown into a rich corpus of hymnody for the church year, and the primary hymns of this sequence occur again and again in Bach's organ works and cantatas."[3]

These chorales were known and loved by the people. "Bach and his fellow countrymen knew German Lutheran chorales as people today might know 'Amazing Grace' or 'O Come, All Ye Faithful.' The chorales were more than simply familiar—they were the music of the people and were important for learning and teaching the rudiments of the Christian faith."[4] Even the presence of just the melody in an organ prelude would evoke the context of the words in the hearts and minds of the congregation. Bach's aim in his sacred vocal music was the edification of the congregation. As such, he wanted his music to be understood; however, it is important to realize that understanding is only part of edification—provoking a more mature discernment and spiritual growth is the other part.

Bach engaged the congregation with words and melodies they already knew, but then he would utilize musical and textual commentary to expand that knowledge. Most of the cantatas open with a straightforward enunciation of the familiar chorale. The subsequent sections offer solos and duets that explain the theological content of the chorale words and develop the theological themes. Bach also developed the melodic themes in these sections by using elements of the original tune. The cantatas close with a simple presentation of the original chorale in such a manner that the congregation could join in singing. As such, the "least interesting" section occurs at the end—not the way to finish with an emotional punch. However, that kind of thinking is antithetical to the concept of Bach's work as a musical sermon that contributed to the overall liturgy. Being biblically appropriate, Bach sought to engage *both* the emotions and the intellect, recognizing that is the way God created man.

This explanation satisfies the notion of Bach's speaking directly and comprehensively to the people of his congregations and era. While the use of specific chorale tunes might seem to suggest that Bach's music is suitable only within a context that easily knows the source material, Bach's works transcend that immediate purpose and are timeless. There are several reasons that explain this phenomenon:

1. People recognize true spirituality and transcendence even if they cannot fully comprehend it.
2. Bach speaks directly to the listener in a winsome way that is erudite but not dry.

3. Bach's technical achievements are such that hearers instinctively respond to his artistry.
4. Bach does not dumb-down his ideas but seeks to raise the understanding of the hearer.
5. There is a universality and breadth to his works that is not easily compartmentalized or relegated to the past.

Johann Nikolaus Forkel wrote in 1802 that "even he who is no connoisseur, who knows no more than the musical alphabet, can hardly refrain from admiration when [Bach's works] are well played to him and when he opens his ear and heart to them without prejudice."[5] Bach successfully bridged the gap between ignorance and erudition, comprehension and immeasurability, the familiar and the extraordinary, poignancy and intelligence. Bach still speaks, and people the world over still respond.

Perpetual Learner

Only he who knows much can teach much.

—Johann Nikolaus Forkel (1749–1818)[6]

B ACH RECEIVED A FIRM foundation of education in his youth in the medieval tradition of the *trivium*—grammar, logic, and rhetoric. However, he sincerely regretted his lack of an opportunity to continue his education at the university level, one of the things he desperately desired for his own sons. His education exceeded that of most of his relatives, and the need to make a living, coupled with the lack of funds, probably inhibited his ability to further his education.

Bach determined that he would continue his education through study on his own—a practice he sustained the rest of his life. The process of furthering his music education, especially in the area of composition, began early, as the story of his copying Christoph's bundle of music by moonlight attests. When he was organist in Arnstadt, he took leave to travel to Lübeck to hear the great organist and composer Buxtehude in order "to comprehend one thing and another about his art."[7] Bach took excursions to hear various organists while in school in Lüneburg. The copying of Italian music during his years in Weimar completed the process of helping him to think musically.

Crucial to his development as a musician was the continuation and furthering of his theological knowledge and understanding, because, for Bach, "theological and musical scholarship were two sides of the same coin: the search for divine revelation, or the quest for God."[8] To that end, Bach had an extensive library of theological works. The inventory of Bach's household completed at the time of his death indicated more than eighty volumes, including two sets of the complete works of Martin Luther as well as other works by Luther, a book on the *Augsburg Confession,* specific works on theological issues, and an eight-volume hymnal.[9] In addition Bach owned two different editions of Luther's sermons for the Sundays and festivals of the church year.[10] Conspicuously missing are musical treatises, which must have been divided among his musical sons at the same time his music scores were separated.[11] "Bach's library indicates that he 'did his homework' and that he would have been able to hold his own in both professional and convivial theological discussions with colleagues and friends."[12]

One of the titles in Bach's library that provides a critical understanding of his study and depth of thought is the *Calovius* three-volume Bible with commentary. Bach added his own markings and comments in the margins, which "reveal not only a careful reader but also a knowledgeable one."[13] As Robin Leaver also points out, "The marginalia and underlinings, written for no one but the Thomaskantor himself, reveal that he was a careful student of the Bible."[14]

Bach maintained a variety of professional and personal relationships with professors from the University of Leipzig. He also taught at least sixty and probably more than one hundred university students during his tenure in Leipzig. Bach surrounded himself with academicians and scholars. His works indicate that he was cognizant, coherent, and responsive to intellectual theories and philosophies of his day. The combination of these scholars and visiting colleagues who frequently sought him out as they passed through town must have made Bach's home a lively haven of discussion and discourse. The coffee, libations, and tobacco would surely have flowed freely.

Bach's musical innovations show a mind continuing to stretch and explore various potentials. From the development of new playing techniques based on ergonomics to the improvements in instrument technology and the extension of organ design—"which required considerable experience in mathematics, physics, acoustics, architecture, and mechanical engineering"[15]—Bach sought the perpetual advance of ability and understanding.

These traits of perpetually learning, constantly expanding knowledge, and applying understanding and wisdom contributed to his legacy and ability as a teacher as well. Forkel observes:

The fatiguing path of self-instruction, on which the learner goes astray a thousand times before he discovers or reaches the goal, is, perhaps, the only one that can produce a perfectly good teacher. The frequent fruitless attempts and errors make him gradually acquainted with the whole domain of art; he discovers every obstacle to his progress, and learns to avoid it. This way is, indeed, the longest; but he who has energy in himself will still accomplish it, and, as a reward for his exertions, learn to find his goal by a way which will be the more agreeable.[16]

The refining of compositional techniques dominated Bach's later years. He moved his compositions into greater and higher levels of unity and strengthened the interrelationships of music, language, rhetoric, poetics, and theology in his art.[17] These summation works show an artist who continued to grow and mature throughout the entirety of his career and who was never satisfied to rest on his laurels.

His legacy is not only that of a musical genius but also an intellectual giant. "For himself and for his ideals, he cultivated the concept of the musician-scholar, or performer-composer."[18]

FAITH

*Bach the Christian, Bach the believer. To
appreciate more fully the character of his music
requires that we more fully appreciate the
character of his faith.[19]*

SINCE THE 1950s, MODERN scholars have sought
to disprove the personal nature of Bach's faith.
In a lecture given in 1962 in East Germany, scholar
Friedrich Blume took direct aim against Bach's religious
beliefs and their connection with his work:

Did Bach have a special liking for church work? Was it a
spiritual necessity for him? Hardly. There is at any rate no
evidence that it was. Bach the supreme cantor, the creative servant of the Word of God, the staunch Lutheran,
is a legend. . . . [N]umerous works, oratorios, masses, and
cantatas, which we have grown deeply to cherish as professions of Christian faith, works [which have] taught us
to revere the great churchman, the mighty Christian her-
ald, have [at the outset] nothing in common with such
values and sentiments and were not written with the

intention of proclaiming the composer's Christian faith, still less from a heartfelt need to do so.[20]

Modern scholars, performers, and audiences cannot ignore the music of Sebastian Bach, but they can attempt to obfuscate his faith and its basis as the foundation of his works. What, therefore, is the foundation on which Bach's Christian faith is best understood?

First, the heart of a man is God's prerogative to know. However, Scripture does say that a regenerate man will bear fruit. From the evidence of the content of his works and the character of his life, Bach bore a consistent witness to the work of the Holy Spirit within him.

Second, the depth of Bach's knowledge and study of Scripture is apparent in the margin notes he made in his personal Bible, the Calov Bible. Listed in the library at the time of his death, this three-volume set contains Martin Luther's German translation of Scripture, along with Luther's exposition of various passages. Bach's personal copy of this Bible surfaced in a Michigan farmhouse in 1934. "The marginalia and underlinings, written for no one but the Thomaskantor himself, reveal that he was a careful student of the Bible."[21] That fact should come as no surprise, considering the careful and instructive manner in which he set Scripture texts to music and used Scripture to comment on other texts.

Third, Bach underwent an extensive objective scrutiny of his understanding of theology and doctrine at the time of his interview for the job in Leipzig. Both a professor of theology at Leipzig University and the senior pastor in Leipzig (also a theology professor at the university) examined Bach—in Latin—concerning his assent to the Lutheran *Book of Concord* and questions related to biblical theology. The *Book of Concord* "is an anthology of confessional documents embracing fundamental Lutheran theology," which contains, as Robin Leaver explains, the concepts of "*sola scriptura, sola gratia* and *sola fide:* that is, one's standing before God rests not with the authority of the church but on the authority of scripture; that one's salvation—or justification, to use Reformation vocabulary—depends upon the grace of God in Christ, rather than on any human endeavor; and that this salvation can only be appropriated by faith."[22] Bach signed a statement indicating that he subscribed to these beliefs and none other.

Fourth, Bach expressed a real and profound hope in eternal life and the resurrection of Christ. He readily identified himself as a sinner in need of God's grace and mercy, and he looked expectantly for redemption.

Fifth, Bach professed his religious fervor in the conscientious manner in which he fulfilled his vocation. As Martin Shannon wrote, "Johann Sebastian Bach expressed his faith and his dedication to God's glory, as well as his mastery of musical concepts, in patterns of sound and harmony."[23]

That Bach's faith was a very real and essential part of his life and work should be apparent to all except those who seek to marginalize the gospel wherever it is found. Bach could not have been the artist he was without an intense and personal relationship with God. It is futile to attempt to divorce his faith from his work, as if man could divide spirit from flesh.

"There is no loftier example in history of artistic genius devoted to the service of religion than we find in Johann Sebastian Bach. He always felt that his life was consecrated to God, to the honor of the Church and the well-being of men."[24]

HUMILITY

Bach was anything but proud of his qualities and never let anyone feel his superiority. On the contrary, he was uncommonly modest, tolerant, and very polite to other musicians.

—CARL PHILIPP EMANUEL BACH[25]

A CHARGE OFTEN LEVELED AGAINST Bach was that he was an argumentative and difficult man with whom to work. The interpretation of historic documents and speculation of personal motives almost always reflect the Romantic, humanistic, or atheistic world view of the various proponents seeking to read their own views in Bach—perhaps even seeking validation. However, the facts point toward a man who was filled with humility, who thought of others, and who rejoiced in the successes of others without envy.

Donald Ferguson states, "He seems to have been remarkably unconcerned with success. There was in him no envy, no shallow personal ambition, no possibility of equivocal dealing which might bring him worldly advantage."[26] And Forkel wrote in his 1802 biography that "as an artist, he was uncommonly modest. . . . When he was sometimes asked how he had contrived to master the art to such a high degree, he generally answered: 'I was obliged to be industrious; whoever is equally industrious will succeed equally well.' He seemed not to lay any stress on his greater natural talents."[27]

In 1717 the famous French clavier player and organist, Louis Marchand, played before the king at Dresden. Bach, employed at the court in Weimar, accepted an invitation to travel to Dresden and engage Marchand in a contest of abilities on the keyboard. Marchand accepted the challenge; however, when the time came for the contest before the king, the large company gathered waited in vain for Marchand to arrive. He had skipped town very early that morning by special coach. Although deprived of the competition, Bach did play for the crowd to great acclaim. However, instead of reveling in the victory, as the obituary states, "our Bach willingly credited Marchand with the reputation of fine and very proper playing."[28]

His sons reported that he never spoke voluntarily about the keyboard contest he was to have had with the French clavier player. As a matter of musical, as well as national, pride, this story in particular could have been a favorite to extol his virtues; however, he chose to treat the narrative modestly.[29] As his son Carl Philipp Emanuel wrote in 1788, his father was not "a challenging musical braggart," and "Bach was anything but proud of his qualities and never let anyone feel his superiority. On the contrary, he was uncommonly modest, tolerant, and very polite to other musicians. The affair with Marchand became known mainly through others; he himself told the story but seldom, and then only when he was urged."[30]

Forkel says that "all the opinions [Bach] expressed of other artists and their works were friendly and equitable. Many works necessarily appeared to him trifling . . . yet he never allowed himself to express a harsh opinion."[31] Carl Philipp Emanuel tells a story that deserves to be reproduced in full:

> A single example of his modesty, of which I was a witness. Bach once received a visit from Hurlebusch, a clavier player and organist who was then quite famous. The latter was prevailed upon to seat himself at the harpsichord; and what did he play for Bach? A printed minuet with variations. Thereupon Bach played very seriously, in his own style. The visitor, impressed with Bach's politeness and friendly reception, made Bach's children a present of his printed sonatas, so that they might, as he said, study them, although Bach's sons were already able to play pieces of a very different kind. Bach smiled to himself, and remained modest and friendly.[32]

G. A. Sorge, a composer and theorist as well as contemporary of Bach, praised Bach for his modesty when he dedicated a collection of keyboard pieces to Bach around 1745. He wrote:

> Many will perhaps be surprised at my boldness in dedicating the present sonatinas to Your Honour, so great and world-famous a virtuoso and prince of clavier players. But they will not be aware that the great musical skill that Your Honour possesses is adorned with a genial disposition and unfeigned love of your neighbour. It is true that

here and there one encounters an excellent artist and a worthy virtuoso; but many of them are so full of conceit and noxious self-regard that they count as nothing all those they can look down on, and set aside completely that love of one's neighbour which is so much needed. I am sure of something altogether different and better from Your Honour.[33]

All of these testimonials from contemporary sources indicate a man who was comfortable with who he was and who did not have to draw attention to himself—especially in a way that would minimize the feelings of someone else. How does such a great genius accomplish all that Bach did while remaining humble? Bach was an artist with a specific calling from God, and he focused all of his creative output to the glory of God. As such, there was no room for ego. His humility is even evident in the famous portrait painted of him in 1746. As Christoph Wolff points out, "In the portrait, Bach the man takes a back seat to his work, and that is how we have always understood him and how we ordinarily see him: compared with his imposing oeuvre, the human being seems of secondary importance."[34]

Bach's work and his relationships with others were always more important than his own ambition.

JUST
PURE AND STRICT TRUTH

*Faithful are the wounds of a friend; profuse are
the kisses of an enemy.*

—PROVERBS 27:6

*B*ACH WAS UNEQUIVOCAL IN his equity and honesty, and he adhered to pure and strict truth even when it was not politically expedient to do so. He did so because he was just.

Johann Nikolaus Forkel wrote in 1802 about Bach's reception of other artists: "All the opinions he expressed of other artists and their works were friendly and equitable. Many works appeared to him trifling, as he was almost always employed exclusively on the sublimer branches of the art, yet he never allowed himself to express a harsh opinion, unless it were to one of his scholars, to whom he thought himself obliged to speak pure and strict truth."[35] Bach was gentle with those who needed it, but he responded justly when assessing work that required an honest critique.

When he formed part of the jury listening to the auditions of prospective organists, Forkel recounts that "he proceeded . . . with so much conscientiousness and impartiality that he seldom added to the number of his friends by it."[36] One such casualty was Adolf Scheib, who applied and auditioned for a position at the St. Nicholas Church in Leipzig. Bach sat on the jury panel and did not give Scheib the job. It was Adolf Scheib who later, perhaps vindictively, harshly criticized Bach and his music in the press in a series of letters and responses that lasted for several years. His father was a famous builder of organs; however, never did Bach allow his feelings or attitude toward the son sway his evaluation of the elder Scheib's handiwork.

Royal courts and churches throughout Bach's area sought after him and paid him well to test and examine their new or rebuilt organs. They knew that he was knowledgeable—but above all, just. The organ was a highly complex and massive "machine." To understand the magnitude of the examiner's task, Christoph Wolff explains that the organ "embodied the science[s] of mechanical engineering, physics (acoustics), chemistry (metallurgy), and mathematics as well as architecture and the handicraft of carpentry and plumbing."[37] It included individual parts made from "all sorts of metal, wood, leather, ivory, cloth, and other materials" and utilized a combination of wind chests, bellows, ranks of pipes, and keyboards to produce sound.[38]

Carl Philipp Emanuel Bach describes his father's approach in scrutinizing an organ:

No one has ever tried out organs as severely and yet at the same time honestly as he. He understood the whole art of organ building in the highest degree. . . . Organists were often terrified when he sat down to play on their organs and drew the stops in his own manner, for they thought that the effect could not be good as he was planning it; but then they gradually heard an effect that astounded them. . . . The first thing he would do in trying an organ was this: he would say, in jest, "Above all I must know whether the organ has good lungs," and, to find out, he would draw out every speaking stop, and play in the fullest and richest possible texture. At this the organ builders would grow quite pale in fright.[39]

Forkel wrote, "He could as little prevail upon himself to praise a bad instrument as a bad organist. He was, therefore, very severe, but always just, in his trials of organs."[40] Bach was thorough in his assessments so that he could honestly and completely attest to the strengths and weaknesses of the instrument. However, he was not simply rough on builders. In fact, "his justice to the organ builders, by the way, went so far that, when he found the work really good and the sum agreed upon too small, so that the builder would evidently have been a loser by his work, he endeavored to induce those who had contracted for it to make a suitable addition, which he, in fact, obtained in several cases."[41] What a testimony to the fairness of all involved that a church or court would agree to pay extra for the quality of their new instrument.

Bach also tested the early version of Gottfried Silbermann's pianoforte—the prototype of the modern piano. As a student of Bach recalled, Bach "praised, indeed admired, its tone; but he complained that it was too weak in the high register and too hard to play. . . . This was taken greatly amiss by Mr. Silbermann, who could not bear to have any fault found in his handiworks. He was therefore angry at Mr. Bach for a long time. And yet his conscience told him that Mr. Bach was not wrong."[42] Silbermann stopped delivery on any new pianofortes and worked for several more years to fix the faults that Bach perceived. In the end, Silbermann fixed the problems and won Bach's approval of the changes he had made.[43]

Bach's word and reputation could be trusted because he was known to speak the truth—even when it was difficult. Cheap praise is meaningless, but just criticism is efficacious.

Law and Grace

Order epitomizes Bach, yet freedom does too.[44]

Now the law came in to increase the trespass, but where sin increased, grace abounded all the more, so that, as sin reigned in death, grace also might reign through righteousness leading to eternal life through Jesus Christ our Lord.

—Romans 5:20–21

*B*ACH DID NOT SHY away from tackling complex and controversial theological topics for the purpose of instruction and edification. Bach was steeped in the theology and practice of the Reformation. The Bach clan was proud of its Lutheran heritage, and the tangible effects of Luther's ideas and teachings pervaded everyday life throughout the courts that made up Germany. Religious instruction was paramount in education.

The primary texts that Bach studied in school were the Bible, the hymnal, and the catechism.[45] Integrated into these subject areas was also the medieval *trivium* of grammar, logic, and rhetoric. The pedagogy of the day included such questions and answers as:

Q: "Why do you go to school?"
A: "So that I may grow up righteous and learned."[46]

That Bach learned his lessons well is evidenced by his ability to pass a rigorous theological screening before securing his position in Leipzig. The fact that the school required such a screening is itself significant.

With the echoes of *sola scriptura, sola gratia,* and *sola fide* resounding in his ears, Bach's music vividly portrays that the authority of Scripture alone is the basis of one's position before God, that grace alone and not man's attempt to fulfill the law is the essence of the gospel, and that salvation comes through faith alone and not works.

Philipp Melanchthon wrote the *Augsburg Confession* in 1530 as one of the first theological declarations of the Reformation. This document remained a critical part of what German Protestants believed. The *Augsburg Confession,* article 4, states:

> Also they teach that men can not be justified [obtain forgiveness of sins and righteousness] before God by their own powers, merits, or works; but are justified freely [of grace] for Christ's sake through faith, when they believe that they are received into favor, and their sins forgiven for Christ's sake, who by his death hath satisfied for our sins. This faith doth God impute for righteousness before him.[47]

Bach frequently appropriated the doctrines of law and grace into his sacred cantatas[48]—his weekly musical sermons that sought to teach and edify the congregation. The apostle Paul teaches in Galatians 3:24–25 that the law of God was given to instruct: "Therefore the law was our tutor to bring us to Christ, that we might be justified by faith. But after faith has come, we are no longer under a tutor" (NKJV). In the book of Romans, chapters 7 and 8, Paul expounds on not the role and necessity of the law but the freedom that comes with grace through faith. According to his Leipzig examination, Bach subscribed to these doctrines as summarized in the *Book of Concord, Epitome 5*:

> We believe, teach, and confess that the distinction between the Law and the Gospel is to be maintained in the Church with great diligence as an especially brilliant light. . . . We believe, teach, and confess that the Law is properly a divine doctrine, which teaches what is right and pleasing to God, and reproves everything that is sin and contrary to God's will. . . . But the Gospel is properly such a doctrine as teaches what man who has not observed the Law, and therefore is condemned by it, is to believe, namely, that Christ has expiated and made satisfaction for all sins, and has obtained and acquired for him, without any merit of his [no merit of the sinner intervening], forgiveness of sins, righteousness that avails before God, and eternal life.[49]

The relationship of these paradoxical doctrines of law and grace are apparent even in the structure and didactic function of many of Bach's cantatas. "In the opening chorus the problem is stated, often in biblical words, that we humans are afflicted in some particular way by the dilemma of sin and stand under the condemnation of the

Law."[50] The sections that follow include arias, which are solos or duets, and recitatives, which are declamatory movements that explore "some of the implications" of being dead in sin, condemned under the law, and in need of a Savior. "Then a movement, often an aria, presents the Gospel answer to the Law questions. Thereafter the mood of both the libretto [text] and music take on the optimism of the Gospel, the final chorale being an emphatic endorsement of the Gospel answer."[51]

Bach indeed preached musical sermons of theological complexity that explored the problem of sin and the need for redemption but also the path of grace and the way that Christ has made to fulfill the law and bring true freedom. These were no vague and sentimental works of dubious religiosity, but rather a firm assertion of the doctrines of grace as outlined in Reformation teachings. Bach's boldness to present difficult truths in a clear yet profound manner serves as an example: "For the time is coming when people will not endure sound teaching, but having itching ears they will accumulate for themselves teachers to suit their own passions, and will turn away from listening to the truth and wander off into myths" (2 Timothy 4:3–4). The church needs to be prepared to respond to this indifference and rebellion regarding the Word of God.

LONG-SUFFERING

Since the best cannot now be engaged one must accept the mediocre.

—LEIPZIG COUNCILLOR PLATZ ON THE RELUCTANT APPROVAL OF ACCEPTING BACH FOR EMPLOYMENT[52]

T O SAY THAT THE working conditions at Leipzig did not meet Bach's expectations would be a serious understatement. Bach was not even the council's first or second choice and was essentially offered the job out of a sense of desperation since the post had been vacant for a year and a half. In addition, the council was divided along principle as to what Bach's job should emphasize—with the pro-Enlightenment members desiring primarily a teacher, while the more biblically minded members wanted to provide for the worship of the town's four churches. Bach was under the authority of three different school, church, and municipal organizational structures, who were at various times at odds with one another. Bach entered his new position already under a cloud.

"By comparison with Telemann and Graupner [the council's first and second choices], Bach appeared to have inferior qualifications. He had no higher academic education, so his educational abilities could be called into doubt."[53]

Bach began his position with an incredible burst of creative energy, writing on average more than a cantata a week for two years. In addition, his magnificent settings of the Passion from John and Matthew are both products of his first four years in Leipzig. However, as Bach clashed with Enlightenment ideas, conflict ensued with his superiors. One such conflict prompted Dr. Jacob Baron, a chancellor and *bürgermeister,* to state that after seven years in Leipzig, Bach "had done nothing" and had shown "little inclination to work."[54]

Bach's frustrations with the situation are apparent in the letter he wrote to his childhood friend Georg Erdmann in 1730. In this letter Bach said that the authorities "are odd, and little interested in music" and that he had met with "almost constant vexation, envy, and harassment."[55] In addition, his remuneration, the quality and availability of instrumentalists, and the ability of the students were all below what he had been led to believe before accepting the position. As Otto Bettmann observed, "Performances in the town's Thomskirche and elsewhere during Bach's time were definitely inferior to what a modern choral or orchestral ensemble has to offer. Even by standards of his time, the instrumental and vocal resources at hand in Leipzig were not of the quality necessary to provide the fine performances he envisioned."[56]

The Reformation ideal of training all students in music for the sake of the church was eroding before the Leipzig Enlightenment forces. Bach noted that since "so many poorly equipped boys, and boys not at all talented for music, have been accepted [into the school] to date[, it] has necessarily caused the music to decline and deteriorate."[57] Consequently, the worship of the town's four churches where these boys provided the music also suffered. Of fifty-four students available, Bach called "17 usable, 20 not yet usable, and 17 unfit."[58] The council began to refer to Bach as their "incorrigible cantor,"[59] and ten days before Good Friday in 1739 abruptly sent a clerk to inform Bach that his scheduled Passion performance was to be canceled.[60]

To add insult to injury, after almost three decades of service to the school and town, the council brought in a candidate to audition for Bach's position just in case he died. This occurred during a short illness Bach suffered in 1749. Bach recovered and continued to serve for another year until his death. The council met one day after his death and hired his replacement a week later.[61]

Bach was buried with no marker or memorial other than disparaging remarks entered into the civic records "regarding his weakness as a cantor and schoolmaster."[62] As Russell Miles relates, "The final official act was one of reprisal. In figuring the customary death benefits for the widow, it was discovered that, back in 1723, Bach had been paid for a full year, but had not assumed his duties until February. That overpayment of twenty-seven years' standing was deducted from Anna Magdalena's honorarium."[63]

Bach's long-suffering is apparent in his patience regarding these constant offenses. He continued to serve, to write, to cultivate the musical environment of Leipzig, and to fulfill the duties for which he had been hired under constant conflict and probably daily interaction with those who committed the offenses. These trials and Bach's perseverance serve as a testimony of God's goodness. As Paul says in Colossians 3:12, "Put on then, as God's chosen ones, holy and beloved, compassion, kindness, humility, meekness, and patience."

PERSEVERANCE FOR WHAT IS RIGHT

*Therefore, my beloved brothers, be steadfast,
immovable, always abounding in the work of the
Lord, knowing that in the Lord your labor is not
in vain.*

—1 CORINTHIANS 15:58

WHEN BACH MOVED TO Leipzig he wanted better educational opportunities for his sons. However, he soon found himself in the middle of controversy concerning the new educational principles of the day. Bach's stand against the erosion of biblical theology by the ideas of the Enlightenment caused him decades of turmoil and strife, but he refused to relinquish his beliefs in the authority of Scripture. After all, as a child of the Reformation, *sola scriptura* was the bedrock of his faith—Scripture alone as the rule and guide for all of life.

During Bach's lifetime a shift occurred regarding the basic assumptions and fundamentals of life. The church was the primary influence in man's life as the center of everything—relationships, the understanding of civic responsibility, the very basis of how one perceived reality was tied to the authority of the Word of God in the embodiment of the church. By the time of Bach's death, the ideas of the Enlightenment—individuality, reason, and the pursuit of secular pleasure—reigned supreme.[64]

The effect on music was profound. As Otto Bettmann explains:

> As the church's influence began to wane, the complex contrapuntal style that Bach practiced was to give way to the free flight of melody: "cheer music" was to take the place of "creed music": "music to play by" gained the upper hand over "music to pray by," which had been the traditional form of music since early medieval times.[65]

This trend resulted in "lighter, more sensual" music.[66] Another casualty of this revolution was the demise of the church cantata as an artistic, theological, and integrated part of the church service. Bach transported the cantata form to new heights, only to have it ignored and deemed obsolete.[67]

The struggle close at hand involved the state of music at the St. Thomas School in Leipzig. When the council decided to hire Bach in 1723, long discussions ensued about the desired job description, with the members divided between an emphasis on teaching versus an emphasis on training students for church services. As a result, "the position of music in the school was under constant threat from Enlightenment principles, which saw value only in the 'relevant,' up-to-date subjects," as John Butt states.[68]

Bach's difficulties only increased when Johann August Ernesti became the rector, or head, of St. Thomas School in 1734. As Malcolm Boyd explains, "He represented not only a new generation but also a completely different philosophy."[69] His aim was to transform the school into "a progressive academy embodying Enlightenment principles. . . . He challenged the basic assumptions of the old curriculum, and in particular the place of music as a handmaid to theology."[70] He was so opposed to music that his new regulations for the school that he wrote in 1773 do not even mention the subject. He degraded Bach's contributions by disparaging the student's efforts to practice musical instruments. He would ask them, "Do *you* want to become a beer-fiddler as well?"[71]

Ernesti implemented a long-term plan of attrition against the role of music in the school. He began by eliminating extra choir activities and then cut the rehearsal hours for the preparation of music for the regular church services. With regard to Bach, "he usurped Bach's prerogative of choir administrator, accused him of neglecting academic duties, and even, at times, impugned his integrity. Bach, of course, struck back with righteous indignation, and the air was filled with acrimonious debate."[72]

Ernesti wanted to force Bach to give up his position, but Bach would not budge. Bach persevered and challenged the world view shift on the basis of biblical authority—even going so far as appealing to the king. A stalemate resulted between the two sides, with minor incursions throughout Bach's remaining years. Bach remained in this hostile and uncooperative environment until his death in 1750.

Around Bach, "other advocates of progressive concepts were charting a course toward a new aesthetic of art which would hold beauty and sensation as paramount.

But the environment in which Bach worked and lived was not conducive to such ideas, nor did he seem to take much interest in them," states Christoph Wolff.[73] Bach realized the difference between innovative ideas within the framework of Christianity and progressive ideas that sought to replace Christianity. Bach stood firm against the spirit of the Enlightenment.

Perseverance on the right path, for what one knows to be true, is not easy. Faced with disapproval, dissent, and discouragement, Bach refused to surrender his principles. As a result he was maligned, marginalized, and minimized. He watched his work erode, his stature diminish, and his efforts be ignored. Yet he persevered. James 1:12 says, "Blessed is the man who remains steadfast under trial, for when he has stood the test he will receive the crown of life, which God has promised to those who love him."

PREPAREDNESS FOR DEATH

We know him as a giant nature in all situations; great and grandiose is also his joy and cheerfulness. But never, we believe, does his art work with fuller energy and abandonment than when his texts express earth-weariness and the longing for the last hour.

—HERMANN KRETZSCHMAR (1848–1924)[74]

*B*ACH WAS NO STRANGER to death. He was constantly surrounded by loss throughout his life, yet his work expresses no bitterness but rather a great hope. Death, resurrection, and the expectation of eternal life form a major theme in much of his work.

By the time Bach was seven years old, two siblings and a cousin who lived with Bach's family had died. Bach's mother and father died six months apart, leaving him an orphan at the age of ten.[75] Bach's first wife bore seven children, of whom only four survived childhood. Within a nine-year time span, Bach lost three children, his wife Maria Barbara, and his two remaining brothers.[76]

Anna Magdalena, Bach's second wife, gave birth during

each of the first seven years in Leipzig—four children did not reach their fourth birthday. During the period from 1726 to 1730, he lost a child in each year but 1729. Of the twenty children Bach had with both of his wives, only nine survived him. What tremendous loss! But what a ministering of the gospel it is that blazes through his compositions—especially the weekly cantatas.

Many of the cantatas deal with the theme of human mortality and the hope of redemption. Richard Viladesau explores how Bach developed this theme throughout his cantata, "Ah, Lord God, When Shall I See Thee?":

> Yet what makes Bach's treatment more than a mere didactic exercise is the spirit in which the whole is presented, for the feeling of the chorale is anything but morbid. Rather, it conveys a sense of peace, joy, comfort, beauty, even in the presence of death. As E. Power Biggs once remarked, Bach looks death in the face and writes cradle songs. Thus for one who hears and understands the text, the music is felt as a profound statement of faith—a positive assertion of hope and joy even in the face of the inevitability of death. The grounds of that hope are made explicit in the remaining sections of the cantata, which meditate on Christ as savior. The believer thus finds here a powerful and moving reminder and reinforcement of the basic attitude of supreme confidence in and abandonment to God.[77]

Sample lines from cantatas include:

> Christ, he is my life,
> Dying is my gain;

To him do I surrender myself,
With joy depart I thither. (Cantata 95)

My fear and distress,
My life and my death
Rest, O dearest God, in thy hands. (Cantata 156)

Come, Thou Sweet Hour of Death. (Cantata 161)

My heart do not be frightened,
God is thy consolation and confidence
And thy soul's life. (Cantata 111)

My soul will rest in Jesus' hand, when earth this body
    covers. (Cantata 127)

Ah, Lord forgive all our guilt,
Help that we may wait with patience,
Until our little-hour comes near,
Also that our faith be ever valiant,
To trust Thy Word firmly,
Until we blessedly fall asleep (Cantata 127)[78]

Bach's assurance of everlasting life and the comfort of hope beyond the grave extended even to his own deathbed. With his eyesight gone, Bach dictated to his son-in-law a prelude for organ on a specific chorale tune. This particular melody was associated with various texts. In fact, Bach wrote a setting of this tune years before, utilizing the words "When we are in the greatest distress."[79] However, on this occasion, so that there could be no misunderstanding, he specified that the title of the text, "Before Your Throne I Now Appear," be written over the music.[80] The opening words are as follows:

> Before your throne I now appear,
> O God, and bid you humbly,
> Turn not your gracious face
> From me, a poor sinner.
> Confer on me a blessed end,
> On the last day awaken me,
> Lord, that I may see you eternally;
> Amen, amen, hear me.[81]

Bach further personalized this final prayer and hope of salvation through the use of a numeric technique in which the name "Bach" equals fourteen and "J. S. Bach" equals forty-one. The version of the chorale he dictated has fourteen notes in the opening lines and a total of forty-one notes in the entire melody.[82] He has declared his readiness to meet God by inserting his name and identifying himself directly with the text. This technique is analogous to Rembrandt's painting his face in a depiction of Christ and the cross or Van Gogh's using his likeness for the face of Lazarus to express a hope in the Resurrection.

As Paul says in 1 Thessalonians 4:13–14: "But we do not want you to be uninformed, brothers, about those who are asleep, that you may not grieve as others do who have no hope. For since we believe that Jesus died and rose again, even so, through Jesus, God will bring with him those who have fallen asleep."

Bach bore a profound witness on how to die rightly

that continues to act as a testimony to not only believers but the world at large. Through his direct and confident confrontation of death, Bach's work persists in testifying to the reason for the hope within him.

Religious Instructor

*Bach's music—like all great religious music—
performs a kind of "apologetic" function by
evoking in the hearer a belief in the beautiful, a
belief in life, and by raising thereby the question of
the grounds of such belief.*[83]

*B*ACH DESIRED THAT HIS music would edify his
congregations and instruct them in the faith.
The presence of so many theological works in his library,
the evidence of his use of these works by margin notes,
and his family pride in their Protestant heritage all point
toward a man steeped in doctrine. The intensive theological examination that Bach passed in order to obtain his
post in Leipzig indicates he had not strayed from the beliefs of his religious training that formed the core of his
early education. Bach's faith was significant and learned.
His sacred works never express a vague religious sentiment, but rather substantive theological and doctrinal
truth for the purpose of religious instruction in order to
convey the hope of the gospel.

On occasion, Bach has been called the Fifth Evangelist
because of his clear proclamation of the Word of God and

for pointing people toward Christ. While Bach would deny such a title, he could not deny his desire to direct people's gaze toward the Savior. "In a Church which values music and loves to sing, the composer may have as much theological influence as the preacher. Not many eighteenth-century preachers taught the Church as much as Johann Sebastian Bach."[84]

The primary means of Bach's instruction was the weekly sacred cantatas. Bach composed around 295 of these works; close to two-fifths of them subsequently disappeared. He wrote 266 of them in Leipzig,[85] including 150 his first two and half years—an astonishing achievement.[86]

The foundation of the cantata was the familiar hymn, or chorale, of the day, which was established by the liturgical elements of the Scripture reading and sermon topic—predetermined by the lectionary. The selected melody appears in many, if not all, sections of the work. Sometimes Bach presents the melody in full, sometimes in short fragments, sometimes in the vocal lines, and other times in the instrumental accompaniment. Sometimes the chorale tune acts as part of a bass line to a vocal solo or duet. Almost all of the cantatas end with a simple, straightforward four-part presentation of the chorale, which the congregation could join in singing. As such, Bach derived or developed the totality of the music in the cantata (as short as twenty minutes and as long as an hour) from one melody line.[87]

The texts for the cantatas came from various sources depending upon their type. Some cantatas have texts derived from only various stanzas of a single hymn. Some cantatas use the hymn text as a starting point and add Bible verses and religious poetry to illustrate and emphasize doctrinal points inherent in the hymn.[88] With this type, the hymn text was generally prominent in the opening and closing sections, with the possibility of interjections alternating with the other sources. Regardless, Bach's purpose was to illustrate and convey biblical truth.

One manner in which Bach sought to express doctrinal elements yet engage the congregation was the principle of *Affekt*—which loosely means "mood, emotion, or passion."[89] Bach diligently endeavored to invest "his texts with the most intense, appropriate music" by carefully suiting "his music to the mood and meaning of the text even in his organ chorales, where the text itself was not presented with the music, though it was familiar to the congregation."[90] As one of his students said, he had been instructed by Bach "to present chorales 'not just offhand but in accordance with the *Affect* of the words.'"[91] In other words, Bach employed text painting such that the music reflected the text in mood and tone color, and often with regard to specific meaning. Terms such as "ascended," "descended," "dance," "sigh," "joy," or "weep" can be directly represented in the music itself. This was a way to emotionally and dramatically engage the congregation in the process of presenting the intellectual content of rich doctrine.

Bach used the cantatas to specifically warn against the dangers of the Enlightenment—especially its elevation of human reason above Scripture. As Eric Chafe explains, in the cantata texts, "reason is described as leading man into taking offense at God's designs and as the enemy of faith;

it is associated with blindness and deafness and the flesh rather than the spirit."[92] Conversely, "references to light in several of the cantatas explain that, theologically, reason belongs to the realm of darkness and the flesh rather than of spiritual enlightenment. . . . Other themes associated with reason appear in Bach's cantatas, such as its opposition to the way of the cross and the necessity of placing God's Word above reason."[93] By using the cantatas as a commentary on the intellectual thoughts of the day, Bach was able to refute these secular notions using the Word of God to confront them specifically through text and music.

Bach's cantatas continue to provide a corrective for secular world views. This is evident in the manner in which modern scholars often ignore the cantatas or, at the very least, disregard the texts. As Calvin Stapert points out, "The emphasis in the canonical Bach is on the instrumental music. The vocal music, of course, is not totally ignored, but the post-Enlightenment mind accepts it only after mentally divorcing the music from the explicitly Christian content of its texts."[94] Various examples of this post-Enlightenment approach include the statement that the texts of the cantatas and Passions "are so insignificant that we need all the beauty of the music to make us forget them,"[95] or that the texts "as a whole tend to be overly sentimental[,] at times even embarrassing."[96] "The reason Bach's cantatas, in the eyes of posterity, moved from the center to the periphery," Stapert writes, "is the post-Enlightenment preference for generic religious feeling over an explicit Christian message. Bach's cantatas do not fit that bill; they are nothing if not explicitly Christian."[97]

Bach intended these musical sermons to be explicit

instruction in theology and a clear presentation of the gospel. As such, they were not only valuable in his own time but continue to be efficacious in subsequent generations. Bach loved the gospel and wrote sacred music for the purpose of conveying that knowledge and encouraging spiritual growth.

Respect for the Office of Authority

For there is no authority except from God, and those that exist have been instituted by God.

—Romans 13:1

$\mathcal{B}$ACH RESPECTED A FUNDAMENTAL difference between his own person and the office in which he was invested. Most of his disputes in Leipzig were not about feeling underappreciated or some moment of artistic temperament. Rather, he sought to uphold the office and authority to which he had been entrusted.

As Michael Marissen writes, "Significantly, nowhere in the surviving documents is there any hint of Bach's feeling that he ought to be appreciated and recognized for his talents rather than for his official position. In his various clashes, Bach does not question the validity of contemporary hierarchies, but, in fact, continually invokes his place in the hierarchy as part of his defense."[98] In his Calov Bible, Bach marked a passage and underlined some portions of the commentary on Matthew 5:26. It reads as follows:

Of course, as we have said, anger is sometimes necessary and proper. But be sure that you use it correctly. You are commanded to get angry, not on your own behalf, but on behalf of your office and of God; you must not confuse the two, your person and your office. As far as your person is concerned, you must not get angry with anyone regardless of the injury he may have done to you. *But where your office requires it, there you must get angry,* even though *no injury has been done to you personally. . . . But if your* brother has *done something* against *you* and *angered you, and then begs your pardon* and stops doing wrong, your anger, too, should disappear. Where does the secret spite come from which you continue to keep in your heart?[99]

One such disagreement had to do with his right to conduct certain services at the university in Leipzig. The university had agreed to allow Johann Gottlieb Görner, organist at St. Nicholas Church, the opportunity to conduct certain services while retaining the "Old Divine Services" for the town cantor—a prerogative that was part of Bach's job as cantor as well as part of the job's compensation. Difficulties arose when there was no clear division of authority or responsibility and when the fees for the services were reduced from that which Bach had been led to expect.[100]

Bach's concern was not just financial but was centered around a clearly defined role and office. When he was refused satisfaction at the local level, he appealed to King Friedrich August I, the university protector, for a resolution. In his letter to the king, he pointed out that the position and fees have "always been connected with the Cantorate of St. Thomas's here, even during the life of my predecessor."[101] He further recounts his attempts to rectify the situation to no avail. This dispute lasted more than two years.

A noteworthy observation lies in the fact that Bach appeared to have no ill feelings or conflict with Görner himself. Bach supported the appointment of Görner as organist at St. Thomas Church in 1729, and the two men would have had to work together with regard to the service music from 1723 to 1750. In addition, Görner was a family friend who was appointed as guardian of Bach's four minor children at the time of his death.[102] Clearly, Bach did not have a personal grudge or disagreement with the person of Görner himself but rather with the office and authority as poorly defined by the university.

Marissen points out that "it may be significant, incidentally, that Bach's most protracted difficulties were with authorities who espoused Enlightenment ideas."[103] Bach's struggle was against a changing philosophy and world view that sought to erode the traditional and biblical view of authority structures. The Enlightenment's dismissal of biblical authority in favor of human institutions would have caused Bach much alarm. His quarrels with Leipzig authorities are characterized by Bach's arguments "that others have improperly assumed the prerogatives that go with his station; [and] it is quite remarkable how forcefully Bach focuses on the nature of his official position."[104]

The entire attitude and respect for authority was, for Bach, theological in nature. He was standing in the line of faith as expressed throughout the history of Christendom.

As Robin Leaver comments, "In the period prior to the French and American Revolutions royalty was understood in theological terms. When Bach and his contemporaries celebrated the earthly majesty of their ruler they did so with the understanding that such dignity is God-given, and that, however imperfectly the ruler may exercise his office, it is the office as embodied by the person, rather than the person alone, that is being celebrated."[105]

If an office was worthy of celebration, it was also important to defend. The dignity of a God-given office was worth the disruption and dissent of what sometimes seemed to be endless quarrels. If Bach had simply been defending his "rights" and his talent, he would appear to be a querulous and egotistical artist; however, his defense and righteous anger on behalf of his office were grounded in a biblical understanding of authority.

KINDNESS
DEFENDER OF THE WEAK

*It is understandable that Bach, who all his life was
a humble and diligent student, should have been
a wise and kindly teacher.*[106]

*B*ACH MANIFESTED A PROFOUND depth of kindness in the manner in which he cared for
others—especially those who were weak or vulnerable.
He exemplified this character trait in his relationship with
needy family members, his private students, and the students at the St. Thomas School in Leipzig.

The Bach family as a whole was replete with numerous
examples of family members caring for one another in the
form of widows, orphans, and extended family. Bach provided a home for his sister-in-law, even after his wife
Maria Barbara died. Other specific examples include training the son of his brother Christoph and providing a home
for his cousin Johann Elias Bach.

Bach was a true champion of his students in their
search for suitable employment. Numerous testimonials
Bach wrote on behalf of these students as part of their

interview process attest to his commitment in helping them secure employment. He would often utilize relationships and his reputation to help sway the various search committees in favor of his students. On behalf of students, Bach wrote:

> I am heartily glad not only to comply with his request [for a testimonial] but also to state in his praise that he has not only acquitted himself well . . . [but] has in general so distinguished himself that I have been impelled not only to entrust the younger members of my family to his conscientious instruction but also to instruct him regularly myself in those things which he did not yet know *in Musicis.*[107]

> I have no doubt God will induce favorably disposed patrons, who will not fail to consider his expertise and provide him, as the occasion arises, with their recommendation to promote his prospects in every possible manner. In sum, he is a disciple of whom I need in no way be ashamed.[108]

> I still recall with the greatest pleasure the gracious confidence that a Most Noble and Most Wise Council . . . placed in my humble self: once when my modest opinion was required in connection with the repair of your organ, and . . . when, by kind invitation, I duly attended in person the acceptance and trial of this organ. This confidence in me makes me so bold as to flatter myself that I shall receive from Your Honors' invaluable favor toward me the granting of a request. . . . For my part I shall count this beneficence shown him as having been granted to myself.[109]

These letters and about two dozen others demonstrate his commitment in helping young musicians find suitable employment by taking advantage of his position and reputation in service of those who needed his help.

Bach also sought to protect the students under his care. The Sunday church services in Leipzig lasted about four hours, starting at 7:00 a.m. The choir sang the cantata in the earlier part of the service. On cold mornings, Bach allowed the choirboys to leave the choir loft after the singing of the cantata. "Cantatas for the winter months are on the whole shorter than those for the other seasons,"[110] indicating that Bach adapted the length of the music for the comfort of the musicians—a practical kindness extended to these defenseless children.

Perhaps one of Bach's greatest acts of kindness toward the defenseless was a long-standing controversy with Rector Ernesti. The complexity of Bach's motivation to intervene included a protection of the St. Thomas students under his care, the guarding of the authority of the office he held, and the security of the worship of the church.

The singers from the St. Thomas School were divided into four choirs that provided the music for the four churches in Leipzig. The cantor, Bach, directed the main choir with the help of a student, the general prefect, who conducted some rehearsals and maintained the discipline of the younger boys. The other three choirs were also under the auspices of student prefects with varying levels of ability according to the required responsibilities.

Bach's job entailed that he choose the prefects for the choirs. However, in 1736 Rector Ernesti removed the general prefect of the first choir "for having chastised one of the younger students too vigorously."[111] In addition, Ernesti expelled him from school and sentenced him to public whipping. The student, who was about to graduate, left town. Angered, Ernesti replaced him with a student Bach did not consider qualified (and who Ernesti himself admitted had moral failings). With his authority to appoint prefects usurped by Ernesti, Bach tried to choose another replacement. However, Ernesti countered by threatening "expulsion and whipping" to anyone who dared to accept Bach's promotion.[112] The conflict quickly escalated and involved multiple council meetings, memos, letters, disruptions during church services, and even an appeal to the king. Records are sketchy as to the outcome, but the affair lasted two years.[113]

Innocent victims in this fray were the students of St. Thomas School and the congregants of the various churches whose worship was disrupted by the political maneuverings and machinations of Ernesti, a champion of Enlightenment ideology bent on reducing the influence of music and theology in the school. The authority of Bach's office was also threatened by Ernesti's seizing of prerogatives and power aimed at punishing Bach and reducing his influence. For the sake of the students, church, and office, he challenged the rector and the council and endured hostile relations with Ernesti for the rest of his life. However, he successfully removed the students and the congregants from the middle of the dispute.

Bach promoted, protected, and provided for the vulnerable and defenseless. He extended great kindness to those who needed his help and depended upon his oversight.

Freedom Through Limitations

The more art is controlled, limited, worked over,
the more it is free.[114]

—Igor Stravinsky

PARADOX IS A BASIC element of the gospel—
life through death; grace and law; losing
one's life in order to find it; the last shall be first. Paradox is part of the fabric of the universe as God created it.
One other seeming gospel contradiction is that there is
the greatest liberty where there is restraint. Freedom
through limitations is a fundamental part of life with numerous applications—especially in the arts.

The concept of a true artist needing to embody libertarian freedom, individuality, free expression, and originality
is a lie from the Romantics. An artist is not an unapproachable prophet who has tapped into a greater reality. A biblical artist is a craftsman who subjugates his or her personal
glory for the greater glory of serving God.

Artists need limitations in order to be creative. A blank
sheet of manuscript, a white canvas, or empty paper can

be daunting without the setting of boundaries. English author G. K. Chesterton expressed these ideas in *Orthodoxy:*

> It is impossible to be an artist and not care for laws and limits. Art is limitation; the essence of every picture is the frame. If you draw a giraffe, you must draw him with a long neck. If, in your bold creative way, you hold yourself free to draw a giraffe with a short neck, you will really find that you are not free to draw a giraffe. The moment you step into a world of facts, you step into a world of limits. . . . The artist loves his limitations: they constitute the thing he is doing. The painter is glad that the canvas is flat. The sculptor is glad that the clay is colourless.[115]

Commenting on these ideas in Chesterton's writings, Thomas C. Peters adds that "the very essence of the arts . . . is limitation, and true creativity involves delineating meaning out of the chaos of experience."[116] Sub-creation, to use a concept articulated by J. R. R. Tolkien, is bringing order to formlessness. It is taking dominion and setting boundaries and limits.

Igor Stravinsky, the great twentieth-century composer and admirer of Bach, explained the role of limitations in his own work when he said, "My freedom will be so much the greater and more meaningful the more narrowly I limit my field of action and the more I surround myself with obstacles. Whatever diminishes constraint diminishes strength. The more constraints one imposes, the more one frees oneself of the chains that shackle the spirit."[117]

The forms in which Bach worked and the development of his musical ideas relied upon the idea of structured freedom. It appears that "Bach savored the challenge of formulating a musical thought that would not just provide the raw material for musical structure but that would define the shape of its individual voices, their interaction, the progress of the piece, and finally the character of the whole."[118] In other words, Bach deliberately crafted musical ideas that would dictate how they could be further developed and how the piece itself would be composed. Carl Philipp Emanuel said of his father that when Bach listened to a complex piece of music with multiple melodic subjects, he knew almost immediately the full range of devices and techniques the composer could employ and ought to utilize. Carl Philipp Emanuel continued by saying that after "he had voiced his surmises to me, he would joyfully nudge me when his expectations were fulfilled."[119]

Bach rejoiced in well-executed structure—his own or someone else's. He credited his study of Vivaldi's compositions as being the catalyst that taught him to think musically. Up until this time he self-professedly flew his fingers along the keyboard until they found some sort of resting place. He learned that musical ideas must submit to order, coherence, and proportion.[120]

The types of music in which Bach excelled, especially the fugue, are some of the most restrictive compositional forms ever devised; however, therein lay the challenge. Bach's artistry and craftsmanship were made manifest not by starting new forms but in his almost perfect realization of the full extent of these existing forms. He reached deeper instead of higher, and by so doing he soared.

True freedom is found in limitations; real liberty is found in bondage to the gospel of Christ.

CRAFTSMANSHIP

The Baroque aesthetic placed craftsmanship above originality.[121]

ABILITY AND TALENT ARE wonderful things, but if an artist does not know the craft of his art, his efforts will ultimately fail. Skill is necessary for craftsmanship, and that requires practice and insight. Exodus 35:30–34 relates several of God's requirements necessary for the artist who was called to build the tabernacle. One of these requirements was craftsmanship: "The Lord has called by name Bezalel the son of Uri, son of Hur, of the tribe of Judah; and he has filled him with the Spirit of God . . . and with all craftsmanship." The concept of craftsmanship is linked to the idea of taking dominion over all the earth as conveyed in the cultural mandate found in Genesis 1:28: "And God blessed them. And God said to them, 'Be fruitful and multiply and fill the earth and subdue it and have dominion over the fish of the sea and over the birds of the heavens and over every living thing that moves on the earth.'"

Exercising authority over the earth does not just entail planting gardens. In the realm of the arts, taking dominion includes movement, language, color, form, and sound as displayed in dance, poetry, painting, sculpture, architecture, and music. Anyone can throw seeds into the ground, but a careful gardener plans, prepares, and cultivates his harvest.

The emphasis in the Baroque period focused on craftsmanship, not originality—an idea associated with Romanticism and Enlightenment views. Certainly an artist was praised for imaginative ideas, but the value of those ideas rested in how the artist treated and developed those ideas, crafting them into something profound. The quality of the idea was dependent on its suitability for development.

Edward Dickinson describes Bach's craftsmanship in this way:

> The material for his purpose was already within his reach. The religious folk-song, freighted with a precious store of memories, was still an essential factor in public and private worship. The art of organ playing had developed a vigorous and pregnant national style in the choral prelude, the fugue, and a host of freer forms. The Passion music and the cantata had recently shown signs of brilliant promise. The Italian solo song was rejoicing in its first flush of conquest on German soil. No one, however, could foresee what might be done with these materials until Bach arose. He gathered them all in his hand, remoulded, blended, enlarged them, touched them with the fire of his genius and his religious passion, and thus produced works of art which . . . are now being adopted

by the world as the most comprehensive symbols in music of the essential Christian faith.[122]

The idea of taking various materials, gathering them, re-molding and blending them, and ultimately enlarging them is the element of order inherent in craftsmanship.

Calvin Stapert makes the connection between Bach's music and rhetoric. Composers "were like orators, making use of whatever rhetorical tools they had available to capture the attention of their listeners and then persuade them of the truth and move them to virtue."[123] Bach's teachers and schools utilized the concept of the medieval *trivium* of grammar, logic, and rhetoric in education. As such, Bach was familiar with the great orators of antiquity and the rules of rhetoric. Deliberately shaping and constructing his music in order to communicate to an audience or congregation was of utmost importance to Bach.

In order for music to be comprehended by its hearers and to "properly affect them," the music should follow the threefold rule of rhetoric as taught in antiquity:

> *Declarare*—"state your thesis clearly and attractively"
> *Explorare*—"vary what you have said, exploring your thesis from different angles, making your audience understand the argument you have advanced"
> *Repetitio*—"return again to what you have stated at the beginning, as to drive home your main point with the force of repetition"[124]

Most of Bach's compositions begin with a simple and lucid musical statement, which is readily apparent to the listener. This clear presentation is followed by an elaboration of the theme in various guises all related to the initial theme. Bach then returns to the original idea for a sense of completion. This concept proves true in a work of a dozen measures for the instruction of his children as well as a choral or orchestral creation of more than two hundred measures.[125]

Bach executed his ideas carefully, meticulously, creatively, comprehensively, and with great craftsmanship. For Bach, taking dominion over the earth meant exercising his calling over notes, melodies, harmonies, and instruments in order to manipulate them to a higher purpose—namely, the edification of the saints and the glory of God.

Natural ability in any realm can be a great blessing, but it is only the starting point. Developing and perfecting a talent is what makes it useful in the service of others. It is not those with great gifts who ultimately succeed, but those who use and improve what gifts they have been given. That is the essence of craftsmanship.

KNOWLEDGE

He had a sheer lust to know and to assimilate all of the music then available, ancient and contemporary.[126]

*B*ACH HAD AN EXTENSIVE knowledge of his art—not only with regard to the artistry of his own works but especially with regard to seeking out, learning, adapting, incorporating, and understanding the works of others. Carl Philipp Emanuel said of his father that he was essentially self-taught as a composer; however, the quality and type of works that Bach created throughout his life show an absorption of the work of others to a degree that shaped and directed his own work.

One of the often-quoted stories from Bach's life concerns the clandestine copying from his older brother Christoph's music library. Whether accurate or not, the story does give the picture of an insatiable appetite for exposure to and knowledge of the work of others—both as a child and throughout his life. One motivation for attending school in Lüneburg might have been the large northern

German organs and their corresponding music. In addition, the four months Bach spent at the feet of Buxtehude—despite his tardy return to his post at Arnstadt—provide further evidence of his yearning for musical opportunities and new experiences.

Bach's second job at Wiemar (1714–17) offered an excellent opportunity to hear different music styles and to have time to work on compositional technique. In his 1802 biography of Bach, Forkel described Bach's early attempts at composition as a "finger composer" who took "both hands as full as all the five fingers will allow, and to proceed in this wild manner till they by chance find a resting place."[127] Forkel goes on to explain that:

> He soon began to feel that the eternal running and leaping led to nothing; that there must be order, connection, and proportion in the thoughts, and that to attain such objects, some kind of guide was necessary. Vivaldi's Concertos for the violin, which were then just published, served him for such a guide. He so often heard them praised as admirable compositions that he conceived the happy idea of arranging them all for his clavier. He studied the chain of ideas, their relation to each other, the variation of the modulations, and many other particulars.[128]

Bach made full use of Italian ideas in his music by incorporating those elements. Christoph Wolff describes the effect of these ideas on Bach as "the coupling of Italianism with complex yet elegant counterpoint, marked by animated interweavings of the inner voices as well as harmonic depth and finesse."[129] These innovations became the most distinctive elements of Bach's own personal style. Wolff goes on to say, "Bach's adaptation, integration, and command of both modern and traditional compositional approaches represent a systematic attempt at shaping and perfecting his personal musical language and expanding its structural possibilities and expressive powers."[130] Bach would never have developed as an artist if he had trusted and developed only his "inner voice." The work and influence of others was necessary.

He often would use a second-rate theme to begin his playing in order to loosen up his own ideas. The concept of improving and crafting art was more important to Bach than the Romanticized ideal of being original. This notion also serves to explain why Bach continued to refine his compositions throughout his lifetime. The application of later knowledge made the refining of earlier ideas necessary.

An artist who remains ignorant of other artists or the history of his art has the potential of being shallow and insignificant. It is the height of arrogance to deny the opportunity of being taught—especially by someone who is already accomplished. Bach showed none of these tendencies and intentionally sought to unify various styles and musical epochs within his own works. The great Mass in B Minor contains various musical styles, contemporary and prior, as well as quotations of chant and elements of Renaissance music. In essence Bach was creating a compendium of music that illustrated the melding of ideas as well as homage to that which had gone before. Otto Bettmann writes that "Bach's willingness to learn from even the least gifted of his associates stood in stark contrast to Beethoven, who was said to have avoided exposure to other composers in order to preserve his own originality."[131]

Exodus 35:30–34 states the qualifications God gave to Bezalel that made him the suitable person to be the creative force behind the construction of the tabernacle. By extension, these are the attributes God bestowed upon him as an artist, and, therefore, these attributes are indications of what a godly artist is. Verse 31 indicates that God "has filled him . . . with knowledge."

The concept of knowledge is not limited to a basic understanding of facts. Understanding of the art form with regard to materials, ideas, usage, concepts, and history makes an artist able to more fully understand his or her place in the history of art as well as to recognize the gifts, personalities, and innovations God had ordained prior to their own time. This perspective also serves to keep one humble.

ORDER AND WISDOM

But thou hast ordered all things by measure, and number and weight.

—WISDOM OF SOLOMON 11:21 (NEB)

*T*HAT BACH STUDIED MATHEMATICS is apparent from the curriculum at his various schools; that Bach grasped the intellectual application of mathematics and order is readily apparent in his works. God is a God of order, as Scripture says. As part of the cultural mandate to subdue the earth, the institution of order is essential to all godly endeavors. Bach took this directive seriously.

Bach viewed music as a branch of the liberal arts *quadrivium*—a viewpoint that was "still as valid as it had been for Johannes Kepler, who promoted the view that music mirrored the harmony of the universe."[132] In 1739 music was defined as "everything that creates harmony, that is, order. And in this sense it is used by those who assert that the whole universe is music."[133] Delving into the intricacies and the interrelationships of order, mathematics, and music was, for Bach, a window to discerning elements of the operations of God and his nature and character. God created math, and part of understanding and exploring math is thinking God's thought after him—some of which can be perceived only through mathematics.

Music is in some ways the aural incarnation of mathematics or a "sounding mathematics," as the Mizler society put it. Mizler's Corresponding Society of the Musical Sciences was founded by one of Bach's former students.[134] Bach joined in 1747 as the fourteenth member. As part of the entrance requirements, Bach composed a riddle canon, which is unsurpassed in its simplicity and gradations of meaning and solutions.

However, for Bach, music was not a dry mathematic theorem and enigma but a living and breathing instrument to reflect the glory of God, who ordered everything by measure, number, and weight, and to serve the nature of man "for the renewal of spirit, mind, and soul."[135]

The forms in which Bach intentionally composed are highly restrictive, controlled, and structured. Part of his genius was the manner in which he utilized those forms to write music that is still ebullient and uninhibited. "It follows, then, that musical structure—*harmonia,* in the terminology of Bach's time—ultimately refers to the order of nature and its divine cause. Or, put more lyrically, 'Music is a mixed mathematical science that concerns the origins, attributes, and distinctives of sound, out of which is cultivated a lovely melody and harmony are made, so that God is honored and praised but mankind is moved to devotion, virtue, joy, and sorrow.'"[136] As Otto Bettmann said, "Every line of music that Bach composed conveys his insistence upon order and his profound faith in God's benevolence."[137]

Bach's compositions, especially canons and fugues, "evoke the analogy of logic or of mathematics; to hear them is to have an inner experience somehow similar to that of proceeding step by step through an elegant geometrical demonstration and feeling the satisfaction of arriving at an inescapable conclusion."[138] This order brings a sense of completeness, of rest. "A Bach fugue ends, as a rule, where it began. This gives Bach's imaginings in sound—whatever mystic heights they may attain—a sense of consoling completeness. Bach always takes us safely home."[139]

One of the reasons that Bach was so skilled at testing new and rebuilt organs was his comprehensive understanding of the relationships between physics, chemistry, geometry, and sound. An anecdote from Bach's son Carl Philipp Emanuel further illustrates this point:

He grasped at first glance any peculiarity of a room. . . . He came to Berlin to visit me; I showed him the new opera house. He perceived at once its virtues and defects (that is, as regards the sound of music in it). I showed him the great dining hall; we went up to the gallery that goes around the upper part of that hall. He looked at the ceiling, and without further investigation made the statement that the architect had here accomplished a remarkable feat, without intending to do so, and without anyone's knowing about it: namely, that if someone went to one corner of the oblong-shaped hall and whispered a few words very softly upward against the wall, a person standing in the corner diagonally opposite, with his face to the wall, would hear quite distinctly what was said, while between them, and in the other parts of the room, no one would hear a sound.[140]

This represents a superior and advanced understanding of all things related to music. This wisdom and discernment had practical applications in knowing how to place an orchestra in a room for maximum effect, rightly tuning instruments, comprehending the idiosyncrasies of the strengths and weaknesses of instruments and writing for or around them, extending the abilities of instruments through modifications, or ascertaining the slightest wrong note even in large groups of performers. These abilities, astounding as they are, were only a by-product of the more essential principle of rightly understanding order as a primary theological concern. Bettmann writes that "the bizarre, the overstated, and world-conquering ambition were foreign to his character. Such impulses are also absent from most of his music, scores that, for all their intricacy, are extremely well disciplined, well ordered, and finely balanced."[141]

Exodus 35:30–34 establishes God's ideal artist for the creation of the tabernacle, "and he has filled him with the Spirit of God, with skill, with intelligence, with knowledge, and with all craftsmanship. . . . And he has inspired him to teach." Intelligence is not just being smart. True wisdom goes much deeper and provides a connection point that links narrow fields of knowledge into broader networks of hitherto unknown complexity and order. All of life ultimately finds its connection in the God of all order.

TEACHER

*Bach's interest and patience in helping young
people is unique among the great composers.*[142]

IN EXODUS 35:30–34, God gives Moses the qualifications of a godly artist as expressed in the life,
ability, and calling of Bezalel. The purpose of singling out
Bezalel was the need for an artist to lead the construction
of the tabernacle. The final attribute mentioned is teaching: "And he has filled him with the Spirit of God, . . . and
he has inspired him to teach." The beauty of a godly
teacher is his desire for his students to surpass his own accomplishments. If one seeks to fulfill his calling to the
glory of God, then passing on what he has learned to the
next generation is a logical extension of that call. It is only
the egotist seeking to be unique who hides the method of
his accomplishments in order to preserve his tricks. As
Bach said, "I was obliged to be industrious; whoever is
equally industrious will succeed equally well."[143]

As such, Bach welcomed the opportunity to teach. As
Christoph Wolff has said, "Bach was one of the most ac-

tive, dedicated, and prolific teachers the world has seen."[144] Students lived with him and his family and even moved with him at various times. While in Leipzig, Bach taught at least sixty university students and possibly more than one hundred. This number is in addition to private students who did not attend the university. "By a conservative estimate, four to six professional-caliber students were working closely with Bach at any given time in Leipzig."[145] As Ulrich Leisinger puts it, "In Leipzig, Bach's talent as a teacher also came to full fruition. No other composer has taught so many pupils who became great musicians."[146] By all accounts, his students were devoted to him throughout the rest of their lives.

Bach was methodical in his approach and provided the opportunity to learn by imitation—a primary pedagogical approach throughout the Middle Ages. As Stephan Daw says, "The concept of learning by immediate example (study by patterns) is, rather, the most ubiquitous form of discipleship."[147] Bach started each student on the process of copying useful compositions, his own and others. And it was his great number of students and this imitative practice that secured his legacy. "If we consider the great number of pupils who were taught by Johann Sebastian Bach after his time in Weimar, many of whom themselves became important musicians and teachers, it is not surprising that large parts of Bach's piano and organ works were very widely distributed throughout the 18th century."[148]

Miles states that "his methods were so thoroughgoing and his standards so high that all but the gifted pupils soon became discouraged. He had no interest in mediocrity, but gave his best efforts to all who combined diligence with talent"[149]—a concept that fits with Bach's quest for the most perfect art to glorify God.

Bach wrote music for his sons and students for the purpose of providing didactic materials that accommodated Bach's own methods and his desired result. The prefaces to several of these works make his intentions plain:

Upright instruction wherein lovers of the clavier, and especially those desirous of learning, are shown a clear way not [only] (1) to learn to play clearly in two voices but also, after further progress, (2) to deal correctly and well with three *obbligato* parts; furthermore, at the same time not [only] to have good *inventions* [ideas] but to develop the same well and, above all, to arrive at a singing style in playing and at the same time to acquire a strong foretaste of composition. [Inventions and Sinfonias][150]

Little Organ Book (with 49 realized chorales), In which a beginner at the organ is given instruction in developing a chorale in many divers ways, and at the same time in acquiring facility in the study of the pedal. . . .

In Praise of the Almighty's will
And for my neighbor's greater skill. [*Orgel-Büchlein*][151]

Keyboard Practice . . . composed for music lovers, to refresh their spirits. [*Clavier-Übung,* Part 1][152]

Daw points out that "many contemporary admirers of Bach were unable to establish a direct studying relationship with him, yet some of these were extremely active as copyists of his music. Some of them made copies in order to instruct their own pupils, some to pursue their researches as students, and others for their own practical use."[153] Just as in his own time, Bach continues to teach generations of pupils he never met but who are willing and ready to submit to the master's instruction.

Most important, Bach did not teach dry technique but passed along life lessons in the application of theology to music. Wolff states that "Bach explored, probed, and taught the principles that govern music—not only its physical, technical side but also its spiritual and emotional dimension."[154] A selfless leader is one who is willing to share his knowledge with future generations for the glory of God.

PERFECTION AND EXCELLENCE

This is the lofty summit of perfection in art which, in the most intimate union of melody and harmony, nobody besides John Sebastian Bach has ever yet attained.

—JOHANN NIKOLAUS FORKEL (1749–1818)[155]

*B*ACH POSSESSED AN IMPULSE to make his work as excellent or perfect as possible. Bach believed that all of life was to be lived to the glory of God. The connection between his sacred or church music and service to God seems obvious. However, he also explicitly revealed this belief in his "secular" works through the creedal statements he wrote on the music scores: "In the Name of Jesus" and "Jesus, help." In addition, his whole basis of rendering accompaniment parts was "in order to make a well-sounding harmony to the Glory of God and the permissible delectation of the spirit; and the aim and final reason, as of all music, so of the thorough bass should be none else but the Glory of God and the recreation of the mind. Where this is not observed, there will be no real music but only a devilish hubbub."[156]

For Bach, there was no secular/sacred dichotomy. Everything was to be done for God's glory alone—all work, all music, tuning instruments, writing keyboard exercises, positioning orchestras, loving his wife, teaching students, dealing with criticism, watching over the care of his students. *Everything!* If all of these things are to the praise of the Most High Almighty God, ought they not to be the very best that can be offered? Should not man seek to perfect his work, excel in his craft, broaden his understanding through wisdom and discernment? Bach fully believed this, and for this reason he sought the correction and improvement of that which he had already accomplished as well as ever-greater heights of new achievement.

"Bach was a tireless corrector of his work, ever trying to improve even the smallest details."[157] The early Bach biographer, Johann Nikolaus Forkel, explained the result of Bach's efforts to improve his works:

> We have spoken several times of the great care with which Bach endeavored all his life long to improve his works. I have had opportunities of comparing together many copies of his principal works, written in different years, and I confess that I have felt both surprise and delight at the means which he employed to make, little by little, the faulty good, the good better, and the better perfect.[158]

Theodor Leberecht Pitschel, an acquaintance of Bach's in Leipzig, wrote about Bach's methods when sitting down to play at the organ. Bach did not start to play his own music until he had "played something from the printed or written page, and [had] set his powers of imagination in motion. . . . The able man . . . usually has to play something from the page that is inferior to his own ideas. And yet his superior ideas are the consequences of those inferior ones."[159] This technique indicates that Bach placed craftsmanship above the idea of individual genius or inspiration. As John Butt puts it, "All music could be the object of his own artistry, it was merely his business—perhaps, even, moral necessity—to improve and perfect the art."[160] Perfection in praise of God was more important than individual achievement.

Butt also suggests how Bach might have defined perfection when he writes, "We get the impression of a composer who believed that every theme and formal strategy brings with it a host of implications that can be realised sequentially or in combination and that the completeness or perfection of any particular piece of music lies in the satisfaction of the entire potential of a musical idea."[161] This impulse in clearly seen in his later "Summa" works—compositions that are the technical and musical summation of various concepts, genres, or musical skills.

Bach's quest for perfection extended to the entirety of his art. "[His] concentrated approach to his work, to reach what was possible in art, pertained to all aspects of music, from theory to composition and from performance to physiology and the technology of instruments."[162] His goal, though ultimately humanly unattainable, was nothing less than striving to love God with all his heart, soul, mind, and strength.

Approaching human endeavors with a godly mind-set of excellence or perfection renders a longevity that transcends their origins and astounds the watching world. Donald Grout expresses this sentiment toward Bach when he writes:

> The continuing vitality of his music is not, of course, due to its historical significance as a summation of the late Baroque, but to the qualities of the music itself; the concentrated and individual themes, the copious musical invention, the balance between harmonic and contrapuntal forces, the strength of rhythm, the clarity of form, the grandeur of proportion, the imaginative use of pictorial and symbolic figures, the intensity of expression always controlled by a ruling architectural idea, the technical perfection of every detail.[163]

Reaching toward what was possibly attainable in his art, striving for perfection, and being satisfied with nothing less than his best could have made Bach a slave to legalism or a tyrant impatient with the performers of his works. The reason this was not the case was that Bach understood the Reformation teaching *sola gratia*—by grace alone. Bach's efforts were a musical offering, a sacrifice of praise, which flowed in grateful response to a loving God. Bach was not trying to win God's favor or notice; he rested comfortably in God's love, and his work was the overwhelmed response of a sinner who knows he has been forgiven. For Bach, perfection and offering God his best were not a burden but a joyful expression of thanksgiving and praise.

SUMMA
REALIZED POTENTIAL

The activity of this man was many-sided, and his
invention seems truly inexhaustible. He touched
every style of music known to his day except the
opera, and most of the forms that he handled he
raised to the highest power that they have ever
attained.[164]

*B*ACH WAS NEVER ONE to leave well enough
alone. He continued to press for ever-greater
accomplishments in his compositional technique, innovations, and achievements. As a result, he left a body of
work that stretched and realized the latent possibilities of
various musical potentials. Donald Jay Grout summarizes
this accomplishment by saying that this goal

is characteristic of Bach's desire to fulfill thoroughly the
potentialities of a given undertaking, to realize all the sug-
gestions inherent in any musical situation. This is the reason that in the maturity of his life his compositions are
often devoted to single aspects of one large unified
design—for example, the complete circle of keys in *The*

Well-Tempered Clavier, the cycle of catechism chorales in the *Clavier Übung,* the systematic order of the *Goldberg Variations,* the exhaustive working out of a single subject in *A Musical Offering,* or the exemplification of all types of fugue in *The Art of Fugue.*[165]

This tendency is known as "summa," and these works are Bach's summation works, because with them he reached the apex of invention and potential.

"Bach had a mania for completeness and for organization. 'He would not suffer anything that was half-finished, unfocussed, impure,' one of his contemporaries, C. F. Crämer, observed."[166] An anecdote from the eighteenth century humorously illustrates this bearing:

Johann Sebastian Bach once came into a large company while a musical amateur was sitting and improvising at a harpsichord. The moment the latter became aware of the presence of the great master, he sprang up and left off with a dissonant chord. Bach, who heard it, was so offended by this musical unpleasantness that he passed right by his host, who was coming to meet him, rushed to the harpsichord, resolved the dissonant chord, and made an appropriate cadence. Only then did he approach his guest and make him his bow of greeting.[167]

Numerous comments and quotations highlight the significance and accomplishment of his summa works. "The culmination of Bach's work as a church musician was reached in his settings of the Passion according to St. John and St. Matthew."[168] Concerning the Mass in B

Minor: "So vast is it in scale, so majestic in its movement, so elemental in the grandeur of its climaxes, that it may well be taken as the loftiest expression in tones of the prophetic faith of Christendom."[169] Of the cantatas: "The choruses of Bach's cantatas would furnish a field for endless study. Nowhere else is his genius more grandly displayed. The only work entitled to be compared with these choruses is found in Handel's oratorios."[170] In reference to *The Art of Fugue:* "Musicians for over 200 years have been awed by the incredible technique and ingenuity with which Bach, in *The Art of the Fugue,* summarized everything known about counterpoint and then added the full measure of his own mighty genius, creating a score that in its majesty and poetry stands unique."[171] Of his organ compositions: "Bach brought the organ chorale to a summit of artistic perfection,"[172] and in his organ works "all types known to the Baroque are represented."[173] *The Well-Tempered Clavier* and the four volumes of the *Clavier-Übung* represent a catalog of various keyboard compositional techniques, innovations, and completeness.

As Otto Bettmann describes it, "Bach's increasing tendency to revise, finalize, and consolidate works previously written hardly indicates that his creative powers were at the time in decline, forcing him to focus on his earlier works. On the contrary, it was his full matured creative genius that Bach now brought to bear—still impelled by the resilient spring of his ambition—as he turned from works written for performance to works that summarized his art in abstract terms."[174]

Thus, Bach brought his personal works to completeness as well as summarizing the styles, forms, and music of previous generations in a manner that extended and codified practical and abstract musical techniques into a form that would persevere to the current day. "Where most composers of his day would confine themselves to the rules, Bach *made* the rules."[175] He developed hitherto unknown potentials in everything he touched: from organs to fugues; from keyboard finger positions to Passions; from compositions for solo instrument to compositions for multiple choirs and instrumental ensembles.

While these elements are in and of themselves an astonishing testimony to his great genius and creativity, the principle remains true on less-grandiose levels. Bach had the ability and foresight to see the inherent possibilities in a given situation and to bring those to fruition. Bach taught students to reach their potentials in playing and composing, he spurred on numerous instrument makers to refine and perfect their craft, and he tended to the education and edification of his congregations through theologically precise and instructive works. Bach did not realize potential only with inorganic compositions but, more important, with people, the image-bearers of God.

WITNESS
THE *ST. MATTHEW PASSION*

*The action is historical, but the reactions are
contemporary, and it is this interaction of past and
present that lends the Passions their powerful
irony and layers of reference.*[176]

PERHAPS THE HEIGHT OF Bach's personal expression of faith that bears a strong witness to the
gospel is the setting of the Passion story from Matthew's
Gospel. The *St. Matthew Passion* is the apex of a long tradition of Passion settings.

In the fourth century, a Spanish nun named Egeria
took a pilgrimage to the Holy Land. One of the foremost
elements in her travel journal was the liturgy and worship
observed in Jerusalem. "Her account of the services held
during Holy Week includes the earliest surviving reference to the chanting of the Passion story."[177] Sometime at
the end of the fourth or beginning of the fifth century, Augustine of Hippo made a reference to this same tradition,
and by the middle of the fifth century, Pope Leo the Great
codified the use of the Passion narrative during Holy

Week. According to his directives, the Passion story from Matthew's Gospel should be chanted in the Masses for Palm Sunday and Wednesday of Holy Week and the Passion narrative from John's Gospel should be utilized on Good Friday. Subsequent changes over the next five hundred years included the addition of the Passion according to Luke on Wednesday and the Mark Passion story on Tuesday of Holy Week.[178]

Calvin Stapert explains how the Passion was sung during medieval times:

> Throughout the Middle Ages the Passion was performed in a chant style consisting mainly of simple recitation formulas. During the Renaissance, composers started to set the Passion story in parts, sometimes setting the entire account in parts but more usually leaving the narrative in chant while reserving part-singing for the words spoken by the groups of people and, sometimes, also for the words of individuals, such as Jesus, Pilate, and Peter.[179]

It was in this context that Bach wrote his Passions for services on Good Friday in Leipzig. The *St. Matthew Passion* was first presented in worship in 1727. The primary text is the biblical narrative as found in the book of Matthew. To that, Bach and his librettists (lyric writers) added reflective comments on the biblical narrative, often in declamatory recitatives, and prayers written as arias for solo voices.[180] The inclusion of familiar chorale, or hymn, tunes enabled the congregation to respond as a corporate body just as the solo arias represented the individual's "meditative response."[181] These chorales also gave a moment of reflective pause in the midst of the unfolding drama.[182]

The text also includes six dialogues between "Zion" and the "Faithful," with Zion representing "the entire Christian church that stretches from the Old Testament to the New Jerusalem" and the Faithful as "the body of believers gathered together in worship."[183] These dialogues occur at significant places and seek to draw the congregation into the Passion story as active participants.

Leonard Bernstein, the influential American composer and conductor, explains, with great rapture, how the opening of the *St. Matthew Passion* works in this regard:

> The orchestral introduction . . . sets the mood of suffering and pain, preparing for the entrance of the chorus which will sing the agonized sorrow of the faithful at the moment of crucifixion. And all this is done in imitation, in canon. "Come, ye Daughters, share my anguish," sing the basses, and they are [imitated] by the tenors [while] the female voices are singing a counter-canon of their own. The resulting richness of all the parts, with the orchestra throbbing beneath, is incomparable.
>
> Then suddenly the chorus breaks into two antiphonal choruses. "See Him!" cries the first one. "Whom?" asks the second. And the first answers: "The Bridegroom see. See Him!" "How?" "So like a Lamb." And then over against all this questioning and answering and throbbing, the voice of a boys' choir sing out the chorale tune, "O Lamb of God Most Holy," piercing through the worldly pain with the icy-clear truth of redemption.[184]

Bach uses musical, harmonic, and dramatic effects to draw attention to the significance of the text. The words of Jesus are accompanied by a "sonic halo" of high strings. This is true for all of his text except for "Eli, Eli, lama sabachthani?" ("My God, My God, why hast thou forsaken me?"). At this point, Bach removed the use of the string halo in an orchestrating move that emphasized the human rather than the divine nature of Christ. Successive uses of the Passion Chorale (most commonly known by the words "O Sacred Head Now Wounded") descend by a half step on each of three occasions, which add greater solemnity as the pitches get lower.[185] The words of individuals are set as solos, with a notable exception being the words of the centurion, "Truly this was the Son of God." Bach set those words as a chorus. As Malcolm Boyd points out, "Bach turns the Centurion's words into a universal affirmation of faith, and at the same time bridges the 2,000 years separating Christ's time from ours."[186] As Donald Jay Grout put it, "Nearly every phrase of the *St. Matthew Passion* affords examples of Bach's genius for merging pictorial musical figures with expressive effects."[187]

Bach filled the entire three hours of this massive work with similar effects designed to highlight the doctrinal significance of the Passion story and to draw the congregant into the narrative for the purpose of edification and instruction. The scope of the work is epic but also very particular, grandiose yet highly personal, objective yet individual. Bach's *St. Matthew Passion* served as a witness to the gospel to his congregation in the eighteenth century, but it continues to serve as a witness to the twenty-first century as well.

DOMESTIC HAPPINESS

*If he had thought fit to travel, he would (as even
one of his enemies has said) have drawn upon
himself the admiration of the whole world. But he
loved a quiet domestic life, constant and
uninterrupted occupation with his art, and was
. . . a man of few wants.*

—JOHANN NIKOLAUS FORKEL (1749–1818)[188]

SEBASTIAN BACH WAS A fortunate man in that he
found love not once in life but twice. Not
much is known about his first wife, Maria Barbara. She
was a distant cousin the same age as Bach and an orphan
as well. As a Bach, she grew up in a musical family. Provi-
dence brought her to Arnstadt to live with an aunt and
uncle in a boardinghouse where Bach already rented
rooms. Their common backgrounds drew them together.

Their thirteen years of marriage coincided with some
of Bach's most fruitful learning periods in composition and
the perfecting of his keyboard skills and techniques. This
period also witnessed the steady progression of a promising career. Together they shared the joy and sorrow of giv-

ing birth to seven children and burying three of them. It is difficult to imagine the sudden shock and grief that awaited Bach when he returned home to the news of Maria Barbara's unexpected illness, death, and burial—all of which occurred while he was traveling with Prince Leopold in the summer of 1720.

As stated before, not much more is known about Maria Barbara. The amount of facts and details concerning Bach's marriage to Anna Magdalena should not be taken as a slight to his first wife. It is natural that since more is known about this later relationship, partiality be given to Anna Magdalena as an excellent helpmeet with regard to abilities, musicianship, and involvement in Bach's life and work. However, there is no evidence to suggest that Bach's marriage and life with Maria Barbara were anything but filled with devotion and affection—in fact, everything points to that end.

Anna Magdalena was sixteen years Bach's junior, and at the age of twenty she took upon herself a widower with four young children—the oldest, Catharina Dorothea, only seven years younger than she. As a court singer, Anna Magdalena worked with Bach professionally and continued to do so after their marriage until their move to Leipzig.

A true meeting of the minds and hearts, Bach lovingly referred to Anna Magdalena throughout his life as *"meine Frau liebste,"* or "my most beloved wife."[189] For her, he compiled two collections of music called *The Little Notebooks for Anna Magdalena.* This compilation consisted of multiple works and empty pages in which were written music by Bach, music he copied, some music she copied, musical exercises and puzzles, and blank pages for future entries over the years. In these books are notations in the handwriting of both Bach and Anna Magdalena, which are quotations as well as original sentiments. Anna Magdalena wrote:

> If now my heart be thine
> as truly thine is mine,
> give thou the world no sign, love.
> No, not the slightest sign,
> for thus the love between us
> will ever stronger grow.
> Rejoicing in the secret
> which we alone will know.

Bach himself wrote:

> Oh how my heart with joy is filled
> To see your beauty blooming,
> Till all my soul with music's thrilled
> My heart with joy overflowing.[190]

Bach's attentiveness to her is manifest in the thoughtful and caring ways he honored her with gifts. The record of these items and their acquisitions exists in the letters of young Johann Elias Bach, cousin and secretary to Sebastian. He writes that when Bach came back from a visit with a colleague he "reported to his beloved wife" that this friend:

> possessed a linnet which, as a result of the skillful instruction of its master, made itself heard in particularly agree-

able singing. Now, since the honored lady my cousin is a
particular lover of such birds . . . I should inquire whether
Your Honor would be of a mind to relinquish this singing
bird to her for a reasonable sum, and to send it to her by
some sure means.[191]

In addition, Elias Bach acknowledged a gift of "six
most beautiful carnation plants," received by Anna Magdalena with great joy through Bach's arrangement. He
continued to expound on her pleasure by stating that "she
values this unmerited gift more highly than children do
their Christmas presents, and tends them with such care
as is usually given to children, lest a single one wither."[192]

As Bettmann writes, "All through the ensuing years,
Anna Magdalena remained the center of the household.
Many testimonies—both from Bach's students and from
relatives who spent time in Leipzig . . . comment upon
Frau Bach's infinite kindness and manifold household
skills."[193] Bach was happy and comfortable at home. He
enjoyed his wife, he enjoyed his children, and he took
pains to ensure their comfort and well-being. A leader is
one who rejoices in the wife of his youth and protects, de-
fends, and cherishes the sanctity of the home.

FAMILY

*[Bach] had also the merit of being an excellent
father, friend, and citizen.*

—JOHANN NIKOLAUS FORKEL (1749–1818)[194]

*B*Y ALL ACCOUNTS AND by any measure, Bach
came from an extraordinary family. The obvious observation is the musical nature of the clan. More
than seventy Bachs were professional musicians. There
also existed great pride in their common ancestor Veit,
who fled religious persecution for his Protestant beliefs.
Common professions provided a unique network that
benefited the entire family. Relatives raised orphaned children in their homes, nephews apprenticed with uncles,
widowed in-laws were provided for, and "when a Bach
improved his [professional] position, he tried to place a
younger relative in the post he was leaving."[195]

Bach embodied many of these family traits: as a child
he learned music from his father and uncle; as an orphan
he lived with his elder brother; as a rising professional he
placed kin in his vacated posts; as a professional he

taught his nephews and cousins. According to Otto Bettmann, "Bach took special pride in taking young relatives into his Leipzig home for musical instruction, hoping that they might go on to a successful career in the family tradition."[196]

As a father, Bach cared for the welfare of his own children. Sadly, of his twenty children, only ten survived to adulthood and only nine survived him. His youngest child, Regina Susanna, was only eight when her father died.

Bach actively spent time with his children. "Bach was never too busy to look after the musical education of his sons, and this ranged from their first lessons in rudiments to finishing studies of virtuoso proportions, most of which he composed especially for them."[197] His desire was for his sons to excel him, but he never pushed them to copy him. He just gave them the proper tools for them to find their own voices. "What is amazing is the zeal and endless devotion with which he devoted himself to the upbringing of his children, musically and otherwise."[198]

Music professions were almost exclusively the domain of males. That he did not neglect his daughters in musical training is apparent from a letter he sent to an old friend in which he mentions the family making music together with his wife and daughter singing.[199] Other family activities included copying scores and music parts and entering pieces of music in the family "Notebooks."

Part of the reason Bach moved to Leipzig was for the sake of his sons' education. His job with Prince Leopold in Cöthen had been the most rewarding position he had held, with the exception of not having the opportunity to pursue writing sacred music. However, events made a potential move attractive. One event was the "lack of space and shortage of teachers" at the Lutheran school his sons attended, which resulted, in one instance, with 117 children being "lumped into one class."[200] In addition, there appeared to be some question as to the theological, educational, and moral fitness of the school's inspector.[201] While desiring to remove his sons from this potentially harmful environment, Bach was also looking ahead to the opportunity of a university education a city like Leipzig would afford his sons—an opportunity he had missed.

The heart of a grieving but devout father is evident in extant letters Bach wrote concerning his son Johann Gottfried Bernhard. Bach had twice helped to secure his son positions playing organ, and had twice helped to settle his bills after he acquired debts and skipped town. Bach wrote to one of Johann Gottfried Bernhard's employers in 1738:

> With what pain and sorrow, however, I frame this reply.
> . . . But now I must learn again, with greatest consternation, that he once more borrowed here and there and did not change his way of living in the slightest, but on the contrary has even absented himself and not given me to date any inkling as to his whereabouts.
>
> What shall I say or do further? Since no admonition or even any loving care and assistance will suffice any more, I must bear my cross in patience and leave my unruly son to God's Mercy alone, doubting not that He will hear my sorrowful pleading and in the end will so work upon him, according to His Holy Will, that he will learn to acknowl-

edge that the lesson is owing wholly and alone to Divine Goodness.[202]

Johann Gottfried Bernhard stayed missing for more than six months before he died in Jena at the age of twenty-four; however, the fact that he was enrolled as a law student at the University of Jena may indicate that he had gotten his life back in order.[203] Of Bach's two oldest sons, Wilhelm Friedemann and Carl Philipp Emanuel, Bach biographer Forkel wrote, "The world knows that they were both great artists; but it perhaps does not know that to the last moment of their lives they never spoke of their father's genius without enthusiasm and reverence."[204]

The well-being and happiness of his family remained at the center of Bach's life. With his composing room as part of the house in Leipzig and with the house connected to the school, there is no doubt that the Bach family spent many hours together day in and day out. Bach's sons also joined him in playing and performing at Zimmermann's Coffeehouse. Ambrosius Bach imprinted upon young Sebastian the legacy and importance of a supportive family, which Bach later modeled and lived before his own children.

FUN

I would be hard put to strike up a friendship with Beethoven. . . . But with Bach, I could sit down comfortably and quaff a stein of beer.

—C. HUBERT H. PARRY

A LEADER IS ONE who knows and appreciates the value of relaxation and a glad heart. It is a misunderstanding to think of fun and leisure as something removed from one's calling or as "doing nothing." People wanted to be around Bach because he was learned, knowledgeable, and fun. Bach showed how a lighthearted spirit can be cultivated even in one's work.

Speaking of Bach's chamber music and secular cantatas, Russell Miles suggests that "when approaching these works, one must dismiss Bach as the serious Cantor of Leipzig, and admit a genial, down-to-earth composer, whose capacity for gaiety and mirth was unbounded. Without exception, the finales of his chamber music reflect *joi de vivre,* and many of his secular cantatas prove that he had a delightful sense of humor."[205]

As Otto Bettmann observed: "In truth, the somber cantor's garb swathed a very dynamic personality—a man with his feet planted solidly on this earth, animated by a decided zest for life. There dwelt in him a free spirit. . . . Even his contemporaries noted that [he] was not averse to 'joining pleasantly in trivial amusement with his fellow men.'"[206] In many of Bach's compositions, a joyous mood of banter prevails. "A typical example is the opening movement of the first *Brandenburg Concerto.* Here Bach intones a strong and simple theme, then reverses and transposes it with obvious abandon. The theme reappears time and again, ingeniously transformed. Bach seems to be having fun—exhibiting his fugal wizardry."[207] Bach spoke of writing two lines of music as if they were two people having a conversation.

Many of Bach's secular cantatas were written for performance at Zimmermann's Coffeehouse in Leipzig—the location of the *Collegium Musicum's* weekly concerts. As more secure trade routes were established with the East, coffeehouses flourished in Europe. By 1700 there were more than three thousand coffeehouses in London as gathering places for talking and reading.[208] Zimmermann's gave Leipzig a place for the town leaders to relax, drink beer, smoke, and listen to music. Bach's predecessor, Johann Kuhnau, defined the purpose of the *Collegium* as "establishing side by side a pleasing harmony of sounds and meeting of the minds."[209]

Two of Bach's secular cantatas bear special mention in this context. The *Coffee Cantata* is a lighthearted look at the abuse of coffee—a concern for moralists of the day. Young Liesgen incurs her father's displeasure over her coffee habit, and he refuses to allow her to marry. Liesgen agrees to give up coffee, but only if she is allowed to choose her husband. She then puts out the word that she will marry only a man who will allow her to drink coffee.[210] The customers at Zimmermann's would have especially enjoyed this theme, and the fact that Bach personally owned multiple coffeepots indicates his own preferences.

The Contest Between Phoebus and Pan is a satirical cantata on new musical trends based on Ovid. Phoebus and Pan compete in a singing contest, and the judge "is given a pair of donkey's ears for mistaking Pan's shallow modern-style aria for true art."[211] Miles describes this work as a "tongue-in-cheek satire, bordering on the burlesque, in which Bach and Picander [the lyric writer] poke fun at certain contemporaries who were outspoken defenders of the trite popular music of the day, as well as critics of Bach's style . . . it was apparent that the humiliating defeat of Pan was a satirical thrust at those who championed banal music. Phoebus' prize song, on the other hand, represented Bach, and we may be sure that he had great fun in pitting his style of writing against the caricature of contemporary taste that he provided for Pan."[212] Just to make sure the audience got the point, Bach introduced a music line in the violins that sounds like the braying of a donkey.

Some of his students said of Bach that "his sober temperament largely drew him to industrious, serious and deep music, but when it seemed necessary he could also think in a more light-hearted and jocular manner, especially in games."[213] This was especially true with regard to musical puzzles. Bach would provide erudite musical riddles to be solved by the recipients. The music he holds in his hand in his 1746 portrait is one such amusement.

The Notebook of Anna Magdalena includes a song about the pleasure of pipe smoking written in a juvenile hand.[214] Anna Magdalena rewrote the melody in a more suitable key, and Bach wrote a more interesting bass line. Thus the frivolity of the piece was enjoyed by multiple family members.

Music historian Roland Gelatt said: "Bach's music gives him away. In the incredible legacy he has left us, he smiles again and again. No composer has ever expressed more winningly the mood of clamorous jubilation, of quiet gladness, of vigorous merriment."[215]

The scowling, brooding, angry Bach of most pictures and statues misrepresents the true nature of this man who loved God and his fellow man. The fact that he was able to express his joy through his work made him even more secure and unwavering in the fulfillment of his calling.

HOSPITALITY

All the more occasion he had to speak with good
people, because his house was perfectly like a
pigeon house with all the coming and going.

—CARL PHILIPP EMANUEL BACH[216]

FROM ALL ACCOUNTS, THE home of Sebastian Bach was an active place. In addition to his family, Bach provided quarters for extended family members, apprentices, and students. Ambrosius Bach, Sebastian's father, set an impressive pattern of caring for disadvantaged and widowed family members, orphans, students, and apprentices within his own home. Sebastian Bach followed that example.

Friedelena Margaretha Bach, the sister of Bach's first wife, Maria Barbara, lived with the household from 1708 until her death in 1729. She continued with the household even after the death of her sister.[217] Numerous students, including nephews, also lived with the family as they studied and worked with Bach. From his days at Mühlhausen up until two months before his death, Bach welcomed and accepted students into his quarters as part of his home. One such student was Johann Elias Bach, Sebastian Bach's kinsman, who stayed with the family for four years acting as secretary while also teaching Bach's younger children. In 1742 Johann Elias wrote a thank-you note to Sebastian Bach, which is a testimony to the hospitality he received:

> Meanwhile, I can positively assure my most highly esteemed Cousin that nevertheless I will not be induced . . . to forget the great kindness I enjoyed for several years in his household, but will on the contrary always remember it with grateful feelings and will, if possible, show myself grateful for it in deeds; and to the same end I will not cease to pray the Almighty daily in warm entreaty for the welfare of Your Honor's whole highly cherished household, and particularly to beg fervently for the lasting health of Your Honor. In the meantime, however, I return with many thanks the Roquelaur [coat] and fur boots most kindly lent me, which benefited me greatly on my journey.[218]

Carl Philipp Emanuel likened the Bach household to a "pigeonry" because of the constant swarm of people in and out.[219] Carl Philipp Emanuel also said of his father in a 1775 letter that "with his many activities he hardly had time for the most necessary correspondence, and accordingly would not indulge in lengthy written exchanges. But he had the more opportunity to talk personally to good people, since his house was like a beehive, and just as full of life. Association with him was pleasant for everyone, and often very edifying."[220] The Bach home was a "convivial and stimulating atmosphere" created by Bach through his taking time to talk and meet with people.[221] "No master of music was apt to pass through this place [Leipzig] without making my father's acquaintance and letting himself be heard by him,"[222] continued the younger Bach. This steady stream of instrumentalists and composers could easily have been seen as a distraction from Bach's more pressing concerns in creating his art, but nowhere does he express that he felt that way. On the contrary, he welcomed the opportunity for the exchange of musical ideas.

Family music making was an obvious feature of home life. In a rare personal letter from 1730, Bach shares with his friend Georg Erdmann a glimpse of domestic life. Speaking of his children, Bach proudly says, "They are all born musicians, and I can assure you that I can already form an ensemble both [vocal] and [instrumental] within my family, particularly since my present wife sings a good, clear soprano, and my eldest daughter, too, joins in not badly."[223]

In addition to rehearsals at home, Bach also hosted small concerts as well. When his eldest son, Wilhelm Friedemann, came for a four-week visit, the occasion was celebrated with several concerts including the talents of other visiting musicians.[224]

The inventory of his estate at the time of Bach's death holds some interesting clues to his habits. Bach owned two silver and three brass coffeepots of various sizes. In addition, he owned a silver teapot, two sugar bowls with spoons, and at least twenty-four place settings of silverware.[225] The value of these items indicates these were household items that were used most likely for the drinking of tea and coffee with friends and the serving of large meals with guests. As Christoph Wolff surmises, "What use would Bach have had for four [tobacco boxes] . . . other than stuffing and smoking a pipe or taking snuff in a gregarious circle of colleagues and friends?"[226]

All of these elements paint a picture of a man who enjoyed people, who made time for people, and who cared for people in his home—despite the rigors and hectic work schedule he maintained. People matter even more than the creation of great art.

APOLOGIA
MENTOR FOR RIGHT WORSHIP

*The common, the trite can never become solemn,
can never excite a sublime feeling; it must,
therefore, in every respect be banished.*

—JOHANN NIKOLAUS FORKEL (1749–1818)[227]

*I*N 1802 JOHANN NIKOLAUS FORKEL, a defender and champion of Sebastian Bach, published a biography titled *On Johann Sebastian Bach's Life, Genius, and Works.* He corresponded and consulted with both Wilhem Friedemann and Carl Philipp Emanuel as he gathered firsthand accounts of their father. He also utilized the genealogy Bach compiled in 1735 and which Carl Philipp Emanuel continued after his death, and the official obituary published in 1754 as source material.[228]

One of the striking features of Forkel's tribute is the relevancy of his comments concerning the music and legacy of Bach. The need to defend the virtues extolled in Bach's works has not diminished with time. The concern over trite, emotive music that Forkel suffered two hundred years ago has not lessened in the intervening years. As such, Forkel's critique of the music of his era and the explanation of Bach's virtues are even more relevant today than they were when they were written. There is no greater commentary on the legacy of Bach than Forkel's own words:

It is certain that if art is to remain an art and not to be degraded into a mere idle amusement, more use must be made of classical works than has been done for some time past. Bach, as the first classic that ever was, or perhaps ever will be, can incontestably perform the most important services in this respect. A person who for some time has studied his works will readily distinguish mere jingle from real music and will show himself a good and well-informed artist in whatever style he may choose in the sequel. The study of classics who, like Bach, have exhausted the whole extent of the art is besides eminently calculated to preserve us from that mere partial knowledge to which the prevailing taste of the day so easily leads. In a word, it would be no less injurious to musical science to throw aside the classics in our art than it would be prejudicial to good taste in literature to banish the study of the Greeks and Romans from our schools. The spirit of the times, which is directed rather to trifles capable of affording immediate though fleeting enjoyment than to what is great and cannot be attained without some pains and even efforts, has, in some places, really led to a proposal, at least, to banish the Greeks and the Romans from our schools, and there can be no doubt but it would be glad to get rid of our musical classics also; for, if we view the matter in its true light, this frivolous spirit must be heartily ashamed of its great poverty, compared with them, and most of all with Bach, who is rich almost to excess.[229]

Forkel continued:

When he wished to express strong emotions, he did not do it, as many do, by striking the keys with great force, but by melodical and harmonical figures, that is, by the internal resources of the art. In this he certainly felt very justly. How can it be the expression of violent passion when a person so beats on his instrument that, with all the hammering and rattling, you cannot hear any note distinctly, much less distinguish one from another?[230]

Louder is not always better, and it is certainly not more spiritual. After all, Elijah admonished the prophets of Baal to be louder in order to get their god's attention.

Many persons are of the opinion that that melody is best which everybody can at once understand and sing . . . I should take the converse of the proposition, and say that the very melody which can be immediately sung by everybody is of the commonest kind.[231]

We owe it to this spirit that Bach's works do not merely please and delight, like what is merely agreeable in art, but irresistibly carry us away with them; that they do not merely surprise us for a moment, but produce effects that become stronger the oftener we hear the works, and the better we become acquainted with them; that the bound-less treasure of ideas heaped up in them, even when we have a thousand times considered them, still leaves us something new, which excites our admiration, and often our astonishment.[232]

One of the greatest compliments that can be applied to art is that it produces stronger effects after repeated exposure rather than just momentary surprise. It is this legacy of greatness inextricably and symbiotically joined with his faith that separates Bach from every other composer and provides a corrective for worship.

INDUSTRY

Study Bach: there you will find everything.

—JOHANNES BRAHMS (1833–97)[233]

INDUSTRY DENOTES DILIGENCE OR an energetic devotion to a task or endeavor. Bach worked persistently and relentlessly with an intense devotion to fulfill obligations and to perfect his art. The physical output he produced is staggering—especially taking into account its uniform expression of skill and quality.

Otto Bettmann states that to reproduce the totality of Bach's hundreds of works would require a music copyist forty years to complete the task.[234] In 1850, the newly formed German Bach Society (*Bach-Gesellschaft*) began the process of publishing the complete known works of Bach, identified as the *Bach Gesant-Ausgabe.* The first volume of ten cantatas appeared in 1851. The forty-sixth, and final, volume appeared in 1900. A new edition of the complete works (*Neue Bach Ausgabe*) was started in

1950. When finished, it will comprise more than one hundred volumes—including forty-six volumes dedicated to the cantatas.[235] The Bach-Archive in Leipzig has "over 7000 books, 8000 musical scores, 4000 sound media, 500 graphics sheets and 90,000 pages of photocopies of handwritten manuscripts and prints by and about Johann Sebastian Bach."[236]

According to his obituary, Bach wrote 295 sacred cantatas (five full annual cycles for each Sunday and holidays), five Passions, hundreds of sacred works for organ, and hundreds more works for keyboard and secular settings. Of the above works, two-fifths of the cantatas are missing as well as three of the five Passions. The number of works lost from other genres is even greater.

Bach's ability to write all of these works was the result of diligent study and mastery of various instruments, keyboard technique, and compositional styles at an early age. He was also a good student who excelled in his studies.

In addition to an active composing schedule, Bach also maintained a heavy workload. "Altogether, the Leipzig churches required fifty-eight cantatas each year, in addition to Passion music for Good Friday, Magnificats at Vespers for three festivals, an annual cantata for the installation of the City Council, and occasional music such as funeral motets and wedding cantatas for which the Cantor received an extra fee."[237] Many of these works Bach wrote himself.

Bach's years in Leipzig also included teaching hundreds of private lessons to scores of students. "By a conservative estimate, four to six professional-caliber students were working closely with Bach at any given time in Leipzig."[238]

Bach's directorship of the *Collegium Musicum* (1729–37, 1739–46?)—a public ensemble composed mostly of university students—required additional rehearsals, compositions, and weekly performances. The ensemble varied in size but consisted frequently of forty players or more. The *Collegium Musicum* performed weekly two-hour concerts at Zimmermann's Coffeehouse, and during his tenure, Bach organized more than five hundred such concerts.[239] During the three annual city fairs, visits from dignitaries, and other celebrations, the ensemble would perform additional concerts—including one that utilized six hundred students carrying torches.[240] Since this was a duty separate from his employment at the St. Thomas School, Bach could not use students to copy music, and so he had to use his children and wife in order to produce the necessary instrumental parts.

Bach also taught four hours a day at the St. Thomas School and was required to make rounds one week a month, which involved waking the students at 5:00 a.m. and leading them in prayers. He made frequent trips to surrounding churches to test organs and write reports on the construction of the instruments. Bach invented and perfected instruments, served as an agent for the selling of keyboards, rented out scores of his music, and acted as his own publisher and distributor of his own works. He placed his sons and students in good positions and still had time to welcome visiting musicians into his home.

By far, Bach's most important goal was the formation of "well-regulated church music." As Edward Dickinson put it, "His declared aim in life was to reform and perfect German church music."[241] To this end he concentrated his compositional efforts—especially after his move to Leipzig. The vast majority of Bach's cantatas were written during a very short period of time—approximately one a week for the first two years he was in Leipzig.[242] Over half of his extant works were written for the church during his first five or six years in Leipzig.[243]

Despite this tremendous work ethic and productivity, Bach did not see anything extraordinary about it. He worked hard, but then that was what was expected of him and what he was called to do. His accomplishment remains astounding. Harold Schonberg writes that "by any measure Bach eclipses all. His vision was greater, his technique unparalleled, his harmonic sense frightening in its power, expression, and ingenuity."[244]

The consistent testimony of his industry is its integrity and excellence. As Dickinson says, "But upon all that Bach attempted—and the amount of his work is no less a marvel than its quality—he affixed the stamp of final and inimitable perfection. We know from testimony that this perfection was the result of thought and unflagging toil."[245]

Innovative

Where most composers of his day would confine
themselves to the rules, Bach made the rules.[246]

*I*T IS ALL TOO easy to accept things the way they
are and even to seek to make improvements to
the status quo. A leader, however, is someone who has
the vision and insight to see things in a different way and
to make innovations. Bach was such a person, as shown
by his creation of new techniques, his invention of new
instruments, his championing of new ideas, and his comprehensive approach to all things.

Bach created the idea of using the thumbs when playing a keyboard instrument. As Russell Miles explains,
"Traditionally, the fingers were extended straight out over
the keys, with the thumb hanging uselessly in front of
them. . . . Bach conceived the idea of curving the fingers,
which automatically brought the thumb in position over
the keys, and added by twenty per cent the number of
digits available."[247] In his 1802 biography, Forkel adds:

Now when Bach began to unite melody and harmony so that even his middle parts did not merely accompany, but had a melody of their own, when he extended the use of keys . . . he was at the same time obliged to contrive another mode of fingering, better adapted to his new methods, and particularly to use the thumb in a manner different from that hitherto employed.[248]

Bach had a considerable interest in the development of new keyboard instruments—especially the lute clavier (a variation of the harpsichord) and the fortepiano (the direct prototype of the modern piano).[249] Bach's former student Johann Friedrich Agricola explains Bach's contributions to the pianoforte:

My Gottfried Silbermann had at first built *two* of these instruments [pianofortes]. One of them was seen and played by the late Capellmeister, Mr. Joh. Sebastian Bach. He praised, indeed admired, its tone; but he complained that it was too weak in the high register and too hard to play [i.e., the action was too heavy]. This was taken greatly amiss by Mr. Silbermann, who could not bear to have any fault found in his handiworks. He was therefore angry at Mr. Bach for a long time. And yet his conscience told him that Mr. Bach was not wrong. He therefore decided—greatly to his credit, be it said—not to deliver any more of these instruments, but instead to think all the harder about how to eliminate the faults Mr. J. S. Bach had observed. He worked for many years on this. . . . Mr. Silbermann also had the laudable ambition to show one of these instruments of his later workmanship to the late

Capellmeister Bach, and have it examined by him; and he received, in turn, complete approval from him.[250]

Bach also developed or encouraged the development of the viola pomposa (a higher-range bass stringed instrument), the oboe d'amore and oboe da caccia (woodwinds), and the contrabassoon.[251]

Due to an idiosyncrasy in how instruments were tuned at this time, it was not possible to play in all keys. Some notes were out of tune in relation to other notes. This also limited the way a composer could harmonize melodies. From around 1700 a theoretical solution to this problem had been considered (called equal or well-tempered tuning), but there had been no practical application. As Christoph Wolff says, "It fell to Bach, who accepted this challenge, to demonstrate the compositional practicability of the new system of twenty-four keys, and he did so on an unparalleled level of compositional refinement and technical perfection."[252] *The Well-Tempered Clavier* instituted the structure of the twenty-four-key system of twelve major and minor keys. Bach wrote two pieces, a prelude and a fugue, in each key, with the theme expressing the key in which they were written. The preludes articulate the keys vertically through the use of a strong chordal structure; the fugues articulate the keys horizontally by an emphasis on linear subjects, which "defines the key."[253]

Other innovations include his development of new techniques for playing the keyboard and the pedals, "taking into account the ergonomics of posture that carried over to other instruments and vocal performance; his intense involvement in musical instrument technology, especially in organ building and design (which required considerable experience in mathematics, physics, acoustics, architecture, and mechanical engineering), . . . and his distinctive contributions to understanding the relationships between music, language, rhetoric, poetics and theology."[254]

Bach also made innovations concerning the voicing of organs, and his comprehensive scope and approach to his compositions were entirely unprecedented. Just because something is new does not make it necessarily better; however, Bach's understanding of his art and craft enabled him to make substantive innovations that helped to further the development of his art.

Legacy

So vital was the current of [Bach's] thought that it became in many respects the source and inspiration of what was best in nineteenth-century music.[255]

*B*ACH'S ADHERENCE TO BIBLICAL and objective standards instilled his music with an ageless quality that secured for him an enduring legacy in succeeding generations. The influence that his work exerted on the subsequent development of art music cannot be underestimated. Among his students and admirers, that recognition came early.

In the preface to the 1752 edition of *The Art of Fugue,* Freidrich Wilhelm Marpurg wrote:

To be an excellent musician and not to appreciate the virtues of the late Bach is a contradiction . . . if one looks into his works, one could also draw the conclusion, taking into consideration everything that has ever come to pass in music past or present, that no one has surpassed him in thorough knowledge of the theory and practice of harmony, or, I may say, in the deep and thoughtful execution of unusual, ingenious ideas, far removed from the ordinary run, and yet spontaneous and natural; I say natural, meaning those ideas which must, by their profundity, their connection, and their organization, meet with the acclaim of any taste, no matter of what country.[256]

Felix Mendelssohn, the great composer and performer, dedicated his life and work to the process of attaining appropriate recognition for Bach and his works. From 1835 until his death in 1847, Mendelssohn conducted the Gewandhaus Orchestra in Leipzig—the direct descendant of Bach's own *Collegium Musicum* at Zimmermann's Coffeehouse.[257] Through his conducting, he reintroduced the corpus of Bach's instrumental works, and on his own time, he gave organ recitals for the purpose of raising money to erect a monument in honor of Bach in Leipzig. There existed no marker, not even a gravestone, to indicate Bach's tenure of twenty-seven years at St. Thomas School.

One of these concerts prompted prominent composer and music critic Robert Schumann to write:

Would that I could record last evening in these pages with golden letters! It was, for a change, a concert for men, a complete whole from beginning to end. Again I thought how we are never at an end with Bach, how he seems to grow more profound the oftener heard.[258]

One of the consequences of Mendelssohn's actions and other influences was the formation of the Bach Society in

Germany in 1849, which was dedicated to publishing the complete works of Bach. This project was not completed until 1900, when the forty-sixth volume was published.[259] Composers and musicians eagerly awaited the release of each new volume. Johannes Brahms (1833–97), the famous German composer, called the publication of Bach's works an event as significant as the unification of Germany under Otto Bismarck in 1871. Brahms commented, "With old Bach there are always surprises and I always learn something new." However, when a new volume of the complete works of Handel arrived, "he is said to have put it on the shelf with the remark: 'It ought to be very interesting. I will go through it as soon as I have time.'"[260]

The difference between Handel and Bach was echoed by others. While no one disputes Handel's fame or his work as a "monument of achievement," his music remains a feat "rather than a stimulus to creation for succeeding generations."[261] One of the differences between the two composers is that Bach's "circumstances compelled him to be practical, and his earnest desire was to give of his best in meeting his practical obligations; but he seems never to have been aware of the immediate advantages to himself which could be gained by propitiating his public. Handel, on the other hand, seems almost to have drawn the breath of musical life from his public."[262]

Richard Wagner, German composer and noted egotist, responded to his exposure to Bach's music by calling him "the musical miracle man that was Sebastian Bach" and found it "impossible to characterize the riches" of the music or its "loftiness and all-comprehending significance."[263]

While generally admired, Bach's music has also contributed to the work of composers directly influenced by his works, including: Wilhelm Friedemann and Carl Philipp Emanuel Bach; Mozart; Beethoven; Schumann; Mendelssohn; Chopin; Brahms; Wagner; Stravinsky; William Walton; Shostakovich; and countless others. Since Bach incorporated and utilized music from the past, he also serves as a bridge, connecting and synthesizing early composers with contemporary artists. He absorbed chant melodies, German chorales (of course!), and the music of Palestrina, Josquin Desprez, Obrecht, Praetorius, Schütz, Albinoni, Buxtehude, Corelli, Couperin, Pachelbel, Reinken, Telemann, and Vivaldi, to name a few.

By thinking multigenerationally and not just composing music for the passing style, Bach created a lasting legacy that is just as relevant and affective as when it was written. Working with a view toward the permanent is a reflection of God's immutability and the covenantal nature of God's action in history and of his people. Fads and fashions pass away, but those things built on the foundation of the Word of God will last.

PATIENCE (REVIVAL)

Whate'er my God ordains is right:
 His holy will abideth;
I will be still whate'er He doth;
 And follow where He guideth;
He is my God; though dark my road,
He holds me that I shall not fall:
 Wherefore to Him I leave it all.

—SAMUEL RADIGAST, 1676 *(WAS GOTT TUT, DAS IST WOHLGETAN)*, TRANS. CATHERINE WINKWORTH, 1863. USED BY J. S. BACH AS THE CHORALE BASIS FOR CANTATAS 98, 99, AND 100

*B*Y FAR, THE LARGEST single element of Bach's creative output is his sacred works. More than half of Bach's roughly one thousand extant compositions are works written for church services. The story goes that Bach and his music were forgotten and neglected until plucked from obscurity in the early nineteenth century. This is mostly true, and to a major degree remains true today.

As a prolific teacher and instructor, Bach's students, with their copies of his keyboard works, disseminated some of his instrumental compositions to succeeding generations. In addition, German pride remembered Bach's reputation as an organist—especially his superiority over other national styles. However, churches and performers ignored Bach's vocal music, of which the vast majority is sacred. The single exception was a few pieces that stayed in the repertoire of the choirs at the St. Thomas School in Leipzig.

The reason for this neglect, as Calvin Stapert suggests, was "the post-Enlightenment preference for generic religious feeling over an explicit Christian message. Bach's cantatas do not fit that bill; they are nothing if not explicitly Christian."[264] Only one of Bach's scared cantatas, "God Is My King," was published during his lifetime, and that was an early work composed in Mühlhausen that was preserved in the town records.[265] Comments from contemporaries indicate that he was already falling out of favor because of his adherence to biblical concepts rather than evolving into the lighter fare of Enlightenment music.

The initial reaction to the *St. Matthew Passion* was not encouraging either. Reports from its first performance in 1727 in Leipzig indicate a "sense of shock or dismay." As people reacted to the start of the music, they were "thrown into the greatest bewilderment . . . and said: 'What will come of this?' An old widow of the nobility said: 'God save us, my children! It's just as one were at an opera-comedy.'"[266]

Through successive generations, small groups of musicians attempted to keep Bach's legacy alive. These efforts found their fruition in the young Lutheran composer and performer Felix Mendelssohn (1809–47). When he was ten years old, Mendelssohn's mother presented him with a copied score of the *St. Matthew Passion.* By the age of eighteen, he was already a famous musician, and he turned his influence toward reviving the Great Passion of Bach after almost one hundred years of neglect. The endeavor took great effort to pull together, with the chorus rehearsals taking almost two years according to some reports.[267] No one had sung music of this magnitude or complexity since the death of Bach.

At the age of twenty, Mendelssohn conducted the performance of the Passion on March 11, 1829, which was described as "like the opening of the gate of a long-closed temple."[268] Because the nearly thousand seats had quickly sold out with a demand for a thousand more, they presented a repeat performance ten days later that also sold out. Subsequent performances in other cities quickly followed. Mendelssohn's sister, Fanny, later commented that the concert hall had "all the air of a church . . . the most solemn devotion pervaded the whole. . . . Never have I felt a holier solemnity vested in a congregation than on that evening."[269]

Mendelssohn succeeded in reviving an interest in Bach that has not abated to this day. Ironically and unfortunately, this renewed interest in Bach's major religious works occurred in the concert hall and not the church. As John Butt explains, "The concert tradition of the nineteenth century gained much of its mystique through a sacralization of the musical experience. Music which pointed towards ultimate perfection, which seemed to encapsulate notions of supreme unity and coherence touched the religious sensibility of the nineteenth century. Indeed it could be argued that the religious depth of Bach's music was more appreciated by the secular concert public of the nineteenth century than it was by the congregations of his own time."[270] The emphasis on Bach's music is slanted heavily in favor of his instrumental works. "The vocal music, of course, is not totally ignored, but the post-Enlightenment mind accepts it only after mentally divorcing the music from the explicitly Christian content of its texts."[271] Although in recent years the cantatas have become available in recordings, they have yet to find a suitable home because they are too religious for the concert stage and too long and liturgically specific for the church.

Bach refused to write music simply to satisfy the tastes and preferences of his time. His faithfulness to his calling meant that he was often marginalized during his life and certainly neglected after his death. However, God's timing is best, and by leaving all in his hands, Bach expressed his confidence in God's sovereignty. Bach sought to execute his work week by week, doing what he knew to be right, and he patiently left the legacy of that work in God's hands. The ageless quality of his work is testimony to Bach's great patience.

Soli Deo Gloria

The melody seemed interlaced with garlands of gold, evoking in me the thought: were life deprived of all trust, all faith, this [Bach] chorale would restore it to me.

—Felix Mendelssohn (1809–47)[272]

BACH MADE NO DISTINCTION between secular and sacred music. All was to be done in such a manner as to bring glory to God. His attitude toward his instrumental compositions was the same as with his church cantatas—all of life is under the dominion of God and should be lived with a view of praising him.

Johannes Tinctoris, a fifteenth-century author, wrote a book on the effects of music that began with the words *Deum delectare, Dei laudes decorare* (To please God, to embellish the praise of God).[273] He was expressing the common view of the Middle Ages for the purpose of all art. He goes on to say, "For it is proper to any artist that he be most satisfied with his work if it be perfect. Wherefore it must be held that God, who has not known a work of imperfection, must be most pleased with the most perfect art since he has created most perfect work himself."[274]

Bach believed the same thing as his predecessors: to strive for perfection or excellence in art is an act of worship and devotion to God. Anything else would be an unworthy sacrifice.

When composing sacred music, Bach began his manuscript score with the letters *J. J.,* which was the abbreviation for *Jesu, Juva* or "Jesus, help." He concluded his scores with the inscription S. D. G., for *Soli Deo Gloria:* "to God alone the glory"—an axiom of the Reformation as well as a true reflection of his desires. However, this religious sentiment was not reserved for only his church music. When writing a volume of instructional pieces for his son Wilhelm Friedemann Bach, he started the manuscript with the designation "I. N. J.," which indicated *In Nomine Jesu* or "in the name of Jesus." Bach's intent and purpose were clear, even in his composition for the sake of teaching as well as in his secular and sacred music.

One of the rudimentary skills a keyboard player needed was the realization of figured (or thorough) bass—in other words, a player would have to create numerous moving harmonic lines in performance that followed basic rules based solely upon a shorthand system of numbers. This was a primary skill emphasized by Bach in the early stages of instruction. However, he saw this act as homage to God no matter whether in a sacred or secular setting. He told his students:

> The thorough bass is the most perfect foundation of music, being played with both hands in such a manner that the left hand plays the notes written down while the right adds consonances and dissonances, in order to

make a well-sounding harmony to the Glory of God and the permissible delectation of the spirit; and the aim and final reason, as of all music, so of the thorough bass should be none else but the Glory of God and the recreation of the mind. Where this is not observed, there will be no real music but only a devilish hubbub.[275]

The important point to realize is that Bach is talking about one of the most basic skills in playing—as if he were saying, Play scales, practice brushstrokes, write vocabulary words with a view toward the eternal, for all work is in the service of God and for his glory.

One element of composition from this time period is the concept of "parody," which means using musical ideas from one context in another context. For example, parody could involve taking a piece of music and changing the text or taking musical ideas and incorporating them into another composition. For the modern mind, parody seems a lesser achievement than original composition; however, the value placed on original work or creativity is an Enlightenment or Romantic ideal—not an element of the Middle Ages or the Baroque period.

Bach commonly reused his musical ideas but recomposed them in such a manner that he improved upon them and made them suitable for the new work. This practice was most commonly observed when Bach reused music he wrote for a ruler's birthday or coronation day for the purpose of a sacred cantata or even the Mass in B Minor. Because the music for these secular occasions would be heard only once, Bach recomposed the music in order to take advantage of the quality of his work for a purpose that would be more permanent. Bach used parody techniques frequently with regard to taking music for secular birthday cantatas and incorporating them into his *Christmas Oratorio.* As Robin Leaver writes, "From Bach's point of view, the celebration of the birthday of a prince is also a celebration of the majesty of God, and therefore the music composed for such an occasion can be reused for the overt praise of the 'royal' birth of the Son of God."[276] Malcolm Boyd points out, "It is worth remarking that Bach's works afford no example of a sacred text replaced by a secular one."[277] Bach's use of parody is always an example of taking a secular work composed to the glory of God and further redeeming it by placing it in service for the purpose of worship.

For Bach, all of life was to be lived as worship—which meant that all of his endeavors, whether for church or for the coffeehouse, were to be realized for God's glory alone. Bach's faithful service did not gain him all the wealth or recognition that could have been his in his lifetime; however, his faithfulness was used by God to create a holy legacy that is all the more authoritative because of his humble service.

PART 3

THE LEGACY OF JOHANN SEBASTIAN BACH

Do not think that old music is outmoded. Just as a beautiful word can never be outmoded, so a beautiful piece of music.

ROBERT SCHUMANN

Last Church Composer

*The tide against elaborate church music and the
rapid decline of the Lutheran musical
establishments was well under way by the time of
Bach's death and, at the end of the eighteenth
century, church music had become one of the
least important areas of musical culture in
Lutheran Germany.[1]*

*I*N A VERY REAL sense, the church has been without
a real composer since the death of Bach. With
the changing secular ideology of the Enlightenment, the
focus of composition shifted from the church to the concert stage, from the sacred to the secular. No longer did
composers see all of life for the purpose of bringing glory
to God as Bach did. No longer did composers see every
element of music as a way to praise God and his handiwork as Bach did. In fact, neither did the church see these
things any longer at all.

The church has accepted the lies of the secular Enlightenment for so long that we moderns do not even question
fundamental elements of the arts and culture. We have

made normal and standard such ideas as the cult of the artist, the dichotomy of ideas and practice, the elevation of individuality, and the role of the arts in general. Bach, his life, and his work stand as a corrective for our myopic and secular view of the arts.

The definition of *art* has become "anything done by an artist." The artist and his personality, his notoriety, and his originality become more important than the actual work he produces. The art is judged not by its intrinsic value but by the fame and celebrity of the artist. This is not the model of a biblical artist. Throughout the history of the church, artists were viewed as craftsmen no different from other craftsmen such as carpenters, cobblers, and barrel wrights. As such, composers and artists often did not sign their works because they saw their work as part of the larger community and not something that was to stand out. If an artist is truly creating for God's glory, then the need for the praise of men is secondary.

As Christians, we have become pragmatists with regard to truth. We believe that truth is most important, but we have little regard for the way in which it is expressed. We sing songs that speak truth but undermine the message of the words by a lack of beauty. The triumvirate of truth, goodness, and beauty is a great curative for narrow thinking because there is a Trinitarian aspect to these three concepts. One cannot understand truth except in its relation to beauty and goodness. One cannot comprehend goodness except in how it relates to truth and beauty, and beauty cannot be apprehended without its correlation to truth and goodness.

Beauty is not the same as "prettiness." The Crucifixion

was not pretty, but it is beautiful as understood in its relation to truth and goodness. Too often, "pretty" art or literature or music is passed off as Christian but without the depth or completeness that truth and goodness require.

Art may tell a truthful story but suffer in goodness and beauty if presented through trivial means—such as flannelgraphs or cartoons. It is secular pragmatism that focuses on the message and forgets the means, that looks at content and disregards form, that follows the narrative and ignores how it is conveyed. What does the church express about God when it sings songs with little or no artistic merit in its lyrics or music? Sure, the words may be true, but is the music true as well? Are they both expressed in an excellent manner? We no longer even know how to think in categories like that.

Because of our general lack of knowledge and understanding, we rely on "experts" to figure things out for us and tell us what to do. An expert is one who has knowledge in a particular field; a wise man is one who understands a variety of areas and is able to interconnect them for the purpose of bringing glory to God. Bach was such a wise man who interlaced his insatiable thirst for knowledge with the gifts God had given him. Bach explored beauty, truth, and goodness on a variety of levels in his work—not just on the narrative or textual level.

Bach was more concerned with being a craftsman who perfected his work to make it as complete as humanly possible for the praise of God. The Enlightenment honored concepts of individuality and originality. Yet originality is *not* a biblical concept. Originality seeks to exalt the individual by doing something new that stands out, that denies what has been done in the past, that gets noticed. More often than not, that which is noticed is the shocking that challenges the very basis of morals. As such, modern original art is disposable because it is always replaced by the next newest original art, which is consumer-based. It intentionally has a short life span for the sake of consumerism.

A biblical artist seeks to exalt God by bringing harmony and dominion to creation in a manner that builds on what has been done in the past and that edifies and reinforces theological truth in the hearts and minds of believers and provides a touchstone of transcendence for nonbelievers searching for meaning. Nonbelievers receive an incomplete and contradictory image of the church and God when what they see is the same as the rest of the world. The greatest witness to a watching and thirsty world is something that looks different from the rest of the world because it is itself opposed to the world and the flesh—that is, the gospel of Christ in all of its truth, goodness, and beauty.

Not since the death of Bach has the church been as interested in developing, sustaining, encouraging, supporting, and employing gifted musicians who have both theological understanding and artistic merit. Because Bach was faithful in his calling as a true biblical artist, he continues to fight against the forces of the Enlightenment and modernity every time one of his works is played.

LASTING LEGACY

It is not a quality, but rather a consequence of its qualities, that Bach's melody never grows old. It remains ever fair and young, like Nature, from which it is derived. Everything that Bach took from the prevailing taste of his time (and mixed into his earlier works) is now antiquated; but where, as in his later works, he developed his melodies from the internal sources of the art itself, without any regard to the dictates of fashion, all is as fresh and as new as it if had been produced but yesterday.[2]

THE PRECEDING QUOTE OCCURS in Johann Nikolaus Forkel's 1802 biography of Bach. He rightly perceived not only the reason for, but also the longevity of, Bach's musical heritage and lasting legacy. Bach's influence on subsequent generations of composers and musicians was profound, expansive, and ubiquitous. Scarcely has any composer, performer, or movement passed in the last 250 years who does not owe a debt to Bach's works.

Despite the celebratory concerts and massive recordings of the complete works issued in conjunction with the

250th anniversary of Bach's death, one must realize the difference between Bach's day and the twenty-first century. The bulk of Bach's oeuvre consists of music written for the church in the context of a worship service for congregants who were intimately familiar with the Lutheran chorales that form the backbone of his works.

The idea of performing "religious" music on the concert stage is a product of the Romantic period, which sought to emphasize vague religiosity and emotionalism through the temple of the communal life. As such, Bach's works are most often performed completely out of context. In addition, Bach's cantatas are most often not even performed—they are too religious for the concert stage and too long or theological for a modern church service. The contemporary understanding of Bach is usually limited to the instrumental works that are "safe" for a pluralistic society. Some musicians may go their whole lives without realizing the extent of Bach's vocal music for the church.

Nevertheless, there continues to be unprecedented interest in Bach's music—even as a means of spreading the gospel in foreign lands. Bach's legacy is founded upon a unique artistry that transcends styles or customs because it is melded with truth, beauty, and goodness that transcend cultures and peoples.

As Donald Grout wrote:

We can begin to understand the central position Bach has in the history of music when we realize, first, that he absorbed into his music the multiplicity of styles and forms current in the early eighteenth century and developed hitherto unsuspected potentialities in every one; and second, that in his music the opposed principles of harmony and counterpoint, melody and polyphony, are maintained in a tense but satisfying equilibrium found in no other composer. The continuing vitality of his music is not, of course, due to its historical significance as a summation of the late Baroque, but to the qualities of the music itself; the concentrated and individual themes, the copious musical invention, the balance between harmonic and contrapuntal forces, the strength of rhythm, the clarity of form, the grandeur of proportion, the imaginative use of pictorial and symbolic figures, the intensity of expression always controlled by a ruling architectural idea, the technical perfection of every detail.[3]

Art that fulfills the biblically objective standard for beauty and excellence will never go out of style, will never become dull, and will never lose its power to instruct, edify, and engage. Furthermore, it will continue to elevate people's thoughts, causing them to marvel at an artistry that is but a reflection of the greater artistry, order, and wisdom of our Creator God. Biblical art is always evangelical because it consciously does not conform to the patterns and customs of this world but is transforming and, therefore, points to the God of all truth, goodness, and beauty. "In this sense Bach's music . . . performs a kind of 'apologetic' function by evoking in the hearer a belief in the beautiful, a belief in life, and by raising thereby the question of the grounds of such belief."[4]

As God is a creative God and beauty is one of his attributes, the concept of beauty is theological. There exist elements of God's character and nature that can be apprehended through only that which is creative and beautiful. The music of Bach provides a view into what true artistry, beauty, and artistic wisdom look like.

Bach's lasting legacy is that of an artist who understood the theological and cultural battles in front of him and chose to dedicate himself to the eternal elements of the gospel, fulfilling the role of a true biblical artist. As a consequence, Bach's work continues to teach, survive, and thrive as a testimony to the glory of God.

THE LESSONS OF LEADERSHIP

- ∞ A leader works for the glory of God alone—*sola dei gloria.*
- ∞ A leader must engage others but then expand their understanding.
- ∞ Craftsmanship entails doing things well and is more prized than originality.
- ∞ A true leader is first a leader at home and preserves the home's sanctity.
- ∞ The family is the primary place of leadership development.
- ∞ A leader extends hospitality and knows that people matter.
- ∞ Having fun and exhibiting a glad heart are essential elements of leadership.
- ∞ A leader's religious convictions are expressed through his work.
- ∞ A leader recognizes the freedom that comes with limitations.
- ∞ A leader is humble.

- A leader is industrious and works hard.

- A leader is someone who has the vision and insight to see things in a different way and to make innovations.

- A leader is just and adheres to pure and strict truth even when it is not politically expedient to do so.

- A leader seeks knowledge and does not rely on individual achievement.

- A leader does not shy away from deeper issues of theology and practice.

- A leader expresses patience in affliction, knowing that the ultimate end is in God's hands.

- Order and wisdom epitomize a true leader.

- A leader strives for perfection for the glory of God.

- A leader continually learns in order to be able to teach others.

- A leader stands for what he knows to be true—especially in the face of adversity.

- A leader respects authority and preserves the institutions God has established.

- A leader is kind in caring for and protecting those in need.

- A leader passes along what he has learned by teaching others.

- A leader knows not only how to live but how to die.

- A leader thinks multigenerationally and leaves a legacy.

NOTES

See Selected Bibliography for bibliographical information.

INTRODUCTION

1. David and Mendel, *New Bach Reader,* 402.

2. Ibid., 421.

PART 1: THE LIFE OF JOHANN SEBASTIAN BACH

1. Westermeyer, *Te Deum,* 240.

2. Boyd, *Bach,* 5.

3. Ibid., 3.

4. David and Mendel, *New Bach Reader,* 283.

5. Ibid.

6. Ibid.

7. Boyd, "Bach Family," 11.

8. Wolff, *Bach,* 16.

9. Dickinson, *Music in the History of the Western Church,* 285.

10. Leaver, "Music and Lutheranism," 40.

11. Ibid., 40–41.

12. Wolff, *Bach,* 13.

13. Ibid., 14.

14. Ibid., 24.

15. Miles, *Bach,* 3–4.

16. David and Mendel, *New Bach Reader,* 4.

17. Wolff, *Bach,* 23.

18. Ibid., 18.

19. Schonberg, *Lives of the Great Composers,* 38.

20. David and Mendel, *New Bach Reader,* 456.

21. Wolff, *Bach,* 18–19.

22. Ibid., 19–20.

23. Ibid., 20.

24. Ibid., 22.

25. Ibid., 23.

26. Ibid., 21.

27. David and Mendel, *New Bach Reader,* 288.

28. Wolff, *Bach,* 30.

29. Boyd, *Bach,* 5.

30. Ibid., 6.

31. Wolff, *Bach,* 26–27.

32. Ibid., 28.

33. Miles, *Bach,* 7–8.

34. Ibid., 8.

35. Wolff, *Bach,* 33.

36. Ibid., 34.

37. Ibid., 34–35.

38. Ibid., 50.

39. Miles, *Bach,* 1.

40. Wolff, *Bach,* 50.
41. Ibid., 35–36.
42. Ibid., 36.
43. Ibid., 37.
44. Boyd, *Bach,* 7–8.
45. Ibid., 9.
46. Wolff, *Bach,* 38–39.
47. David and Mendel, *New Bach Reader,* 426.
48. Ibid., 425–26.
49. Ibid., 299.
50. Miles, *Bach,* 10.
51. Wolff, *Bach,* 37.
52. Ibid., 43.
53. Ibid., 48.
54. Miles, *Bach,* 13.
55. David and Mendel, *New Bach Reader,* 126.
56. Miles, *Bach,* 13.
57. Ibid., 12.
58. Wolff, *Bach,* 53.
59. Ibid., 54.
60. Ibid., 55.
61. Miles, *Bach,* 13.
62. Ibid.
63. Boyd, *Bach,* 13.
64. Miles, *Bach,* 13.
65. Boyd, *Bach,* 14.
66. Wolff, *Bach,* 58.
67. Miles, *Bach,* 13–14.
68. David and Mendel, *New Bach Reader,* 426.
69. Miles, *Bach,* 14–15.
70. David and Mendel, *New Bach Reader,* 9.
71. Miles, *Bach,* 14–15.
72. David and Mendel, *New Bach Reader,* 409.
73. Miles, *Bach,* 15.
74. Ibid., 17.
75. Boyd, *Bach,* 15.
76. Wolff, *Bach,* 68.
77. Miles, *Bach,* 17.
78. David and Mendel, *New Bach Reader,* 47.
79. Boyd, *Bach,* 17–18.
80. Wolff, *Bach,* 77–78.
81. Boyd, *Bach,* 17–19.
82. Miles, *Bach,* 20.
83. Wolff, *Bach,* 79.
84. Ibid., 82.
85. Ibid., 80, 81, 92.
86. Ibid., 81.
87. Miles, *Bach,* 20.
88. Boyd, *Bach,* 21.
89. David and Mendel, *New Bach Reader,* 45.
90. Miles, *Bach,* 26.
91. Wolff, *Bach,* 95–96.
92. Ferguson, *History of Musical Thought,* 306.
93. Wolff, *Bach,* 97.
94. Miles, *Bach,* 26–27.
95. Ibid., 26.
96. Boyd, "Bach Family," 14.
97. Boyd, *Bach,* 22.

98. Miles, *Bach,* 25.
99. Ibid., 27.
100. David and Mendel, *New Bach Reader,* 46.
101. Ibid., 47.
102. Miles, *Bach,* 26–28.
103. Ferguson, *History of Musical Thought,* 306.
104. Dickinson, *Music in the History of the Western Church,* 283.
105. Boyd, *Bach,* 23.
106. Wolff, *Bach,* 104.
107. Miles, *Bach,* 29–30.
108. David and Mendel, *New Bach Reader,* 49–50.
109. Wolff, *Bach,* 104–5.
110. Miles, *Bach,* 29.
111. Wolff, *Bach,* 91.
112. Ibid., 107.
113. David and Mendel, *New Bach Reader,* 52.
114. Miles, *Bach,* 31.
115. Stapert, *My Only Comfort,* 20.
116. Miles, *Bach,* 31–32.
117. Ibid., 31.
118. David, 57.
119. Ibid.
120. Spitta, *Bach,* 1:357.
121. Boyd, 26.
122. Shannon, "'Soli Deo Gloria,'" 43.
123. David and Mendel, *New Bach Reader,* 57.
124. Wolff, *Bach,* 471.
125. David and Mendel, *New Bach Reader,* 427.
126. Miles, *Bach,* 35.
127. Wolff, *Bach,* 118.
128. Ibid., 117, 125.
129. Miles, *Bach,* 35–36.
130. Wolff, *Bach,* 118.
131. Ibid., 119.
132. Ibid., 122–23.
133. Ibid., 122.
134. Ibid., 119–20.
135. Ibid., 134–35.
136. David and Mendel, *New Bach Reader,* 70.
137. Wolff, *Bach,* 147–48.
138. Ibid., 155.
139. Ibid., 169.
140. Miles, *Bach,* 39.
141. David and Mendel, *New Bach Reader,* 300.
142. Wolff, *Bach,* 137.
143. David and Mendel, *New Bach Reader,* 306–7.
144. Wolff, *Bach,* 142.
145. Ibid.
146. David and Mendel, *New Bach Reader,* 306.
147. Ibid., 439.
148. Ibid., 437.
149. Ibid., 437–38.

150. Boyd, *Bach,* 49.
151. Ibid., 53.
152. David and Mendel, *New Bach Reader,* 80.
153. Dickinson, *Music in the History of the Western Church,* 295.
154. Ibid., 296.
155. David and Mendel, *New Bach Reader,* 440.
156. Wolff, *Bach,* 174.
157. Boyd, *Bach,* 14.
158. Wolff, *Bach,* 161.
159. Ibid., 166.
160. Ibid.
161. Grout, *History of Western Music,* 416–17.
162. Miles, *Bach,* 38.
163. David and Mendel, *New Bach Reader,* 441–42.
164. Wolff, *Bach,* 173.
165. Ibid., 176.
166. Ibid., 177.
167. Boyd, *Bach,* 42.
168. Wolff, *Bach,* 164.
169. Boyd, *Bach,* 42–43.
170. Miles, *Bach,* 49.
171. Boyd, *Bach,* 42–43.
172. David and Mendel, *New Bach Reader,* 80.
173. Wolff, *Bach,* 184.
174. Ferguson, *History of Musical Thought,* 307.
175. Wolff, *Bach,* 188–89.
176. Ibid., 207.
177. Ibid., 188.
178. Ibid., 191.
179. Miles, *Bach,* 57–58.
180. Boyd, *Bach,* 70.
181. Wolff, *Bach,* 191.
182. Ibid., 194–95.
183. Ibid., 195.
184. Ibid., 200.
185. Ibid., 202.
186. Ibid., 210.
187. Boyd, *Bach,* 72–73.
188. Miles, *Bach,* 62.
189. Ibid., 62–63.
190. Boyd, *Bach,* 72–74.
191. Miles, *Bach,* 74.
192. Ibid., 85.
193. Wolff, *Bach,* 202–3.
194. Boyd, *Bach,* 76–77.
195. Leisinger, *Bach in Leipzig,* 12.
196. Wolff, *Bach,* 471.
197. Miles, *Bach,* 52.
198. Grout, *History of Western Music,* 423.
199. Ibid.
200. Miles, *Bach,* 79.
201. Ibid., 81.
202. Ibid., 53–54.
203. Wolff, *Bach,* 232.
204. Miles, *Bach,* 73.
205. Ibid.

206. Wolff, *Bach,* 232.
207. Ibid.
208. Dickinson, *Music in the History of the Western Church,* 283.
209. David and Mendel, *New Bach Reader,* 106.
210. Wolff, *Bach,* 242.
211. Ibid.
212. Boyd, *Bach,* 110.
213. Wolff, *Bach,* 238.
214. Ibid., 239.
215. Ibid., 237.
216. Boyd, "Bach Family," 13.
217. Leaver, "Music and Lutheranism," 42.
218. Ibid.
219. Leisinger, *Bach in Leipzig,* 25–26.
220. Wolff, *Bach,* 227.
221. Boyd, *Bach,* 112.
222. Miles, *Bach,* 89.
223. Wolff, *Bach,* 248.
224. Miles, *Bach,* 91.
225. Boyd, *Bach,* 112.
226. Ibid., 111.
227. Miles, *Bach,* 88–89.
228. Leisinger, *Bach in Leipzig,* 27.
229. Ibid., 15.
230. Ibid.
231. Grout, *History of Western Music,* 432.
232. Wolff, *Bach,* 250–51.
233. Ibid., 253.
234. Leisinger, *Bach in Leipzig,* 59–61.
235. David and Mendel, *New Bach Reader,* 152.
236. Ibid.
237. Shannon, "'Soli Deo Gloria,'" 41.
238. Leaver, "Mature Vocal Works," 88.
239. Dickinson, *Music in the History of the Western Church,* 304.
240. Wolff, *Bach,* 410.
241. Ibid., 255.
242. Ibid.
243. Leaver, "Music and Lutheranism," 45.
244. Stapert, *My Only Comfort,* 4–5.
245. Wolff, *Bach,* 389.
246. Boyd, *Bach,* 163.
247. Ibid.
248. Wolff, *Bach,* 342.
249. Boyd, *Bach,* 163.
250. David and Mendel, *New Bach Reader,* 328–29.
251. Miles, *Bach,* 114.
252. Leisinger, *Bach in Leipzig,* 29.
253. Boyd, *Bach,* 166.
254. David and Mendel, *New Bach Reader,* 188.

255. Ibid.
256. Boyd, *Bach,* 167.
257. Ibid., 168.
258. Ibid.
259. Miles, *Bach,* 122.
260. Butt, "Historical Perspective and Introduction," 2.
261. Miles, *Bach,* 130.
262. Wolff, *Bach,* 375.
263. Grout, *History of Western Music,* 418.
264. Boyd, *Bach,* 173.
265. Boyd, *Bach,* 229.
266. Wolff, *Bach,* 402–6.
267. Miles, *Bach,* 146.
268. Wolff, *Bach,* 407.
269. Leisinger, *Bach in Leipzig,* 66.
270. Ibid., 22.
271. Ibid., 23.
272. David and Mendel, *New Bach Reader,* 400.
273. Wolff, *Bach,* 411–12.
274. David and Mendel, *New Bach Reader,* 23.
275. Ibid., 204.
276. Wolff, *Bach,* 417–18.
277. Ibid., 418.
278. Boyd, *Bach,* 205.
279. Ibid.
280. Wolff, *Bach,* 422.
281. Miles, *Bach,* 152–53.
282. Butt, "Bach's Metaphysics of Music," 46.
283. Ibid., 48.
284. David and Mendel, *New Bach Reader,* 305.
285. Ibid., 429.
286. Boyd, *Bach,* 203.
287. David and Mendel, *New Bach Reader,* 429–30.
288. Wolff, *Bach,* 430.
289. Dickinson, *Music in the History of the Western Church,* 313.
290. Leaver, "Mature Vocal Works," 116.
291. Ibid., 111–12.
292. Dickinson, *Music in the History of the Western Church,* 314.
293. Schonberg, *Lives of the Great Composers,* 48.
294. David and Mendel, *New Bach Reader,* 23.
295. Ibid., 449.
296. Grout, *History of Western Music,* 416.
297. David and Mendel, *New Bach Reader,* 240.
298. Ibid., 303.
299. Ibid.
300. Wolff, *Bach,* 449–50.
301. Ibid., 451–53.
302. David and Mendel, *New Bach Reader,* 244–45.
303. Boyd, *Bach,* 209.

304. Miles, *Bach,* 162–63.

305. Wolff, *Bach,* 458–59.

306. Boyd, "Bach Family," 16.

307. David and Mendel, *New Bach Reader,* 378–79.

PART 2: THE CHARACTER OF JOHANN SEBASTIAN BACH

1. Boyd, *Bach,* 244–45.

2. Grout, *History of Western Music,* 252.

3. Leaver, "Music and Lutheranism," 43.

4. Jordan, "Lutheran Chorale," 35.

5. David and Mendel, *New Bach Reader,* 478.

6. Ibid., 453.

7. Wolff, *Bach,* 96.

8. Ibid., 335.

9. David and Mendel, *New Bach Reader,* 253–54.

10. Leaver, "Music and Lutheranism," 40.

11. Wolff, *Bach,* 456–57.

12. Stapert, *My Only Comfort,* 9.

13. Ibid., 11.

14. Leaver, "Music and Lutheranism," 39.

15. Wolff, *Bach,* 8.

16. David and Mendel, *New Bach Reader,* 452–53.

17. Ibid.

18. Wolff, *Bach,* 305.

19. Shannon, "'Soli Deo Gloria,'" 41.

20. Blume, "Outline of a New Picture of Bach," 219–20.

21. Leaver, "Music and Lutheranism," 39.

22. Ibid., 37–38.

23. Shannon, "'Soli Deo Gloria,'" 41.

24. Dickinson, *Music in the History of the Western Church,* 314.

25. David and Mendel, *New Bach Reader,* 459.

26. Ferguson, *History of Musical Thought,* 304.

27. David and Mendel, *New Bach Reader,* 459.

28. Wolff, *Bach,* 180–81.

29. David and Mendel, *New Bach Reader,* 459.

30. Ibid., 408.

31. Ibid., 459.

32. Ibid., 408.

33. Boyd, *Bach,* 230.

34. Wolff, *Bach,* 391–92.
35. David and Mendel, *New Bach Reader,* 459.
36. Ibid., 440.
37. Wolff, *Bach,* 142.
38. Ibid.
39. David and Mendel, *New Bach Reader,* 396.
40. Ibid., 440.
41. Ibid., 441.
42. Ibid., 365–66.
43. Ibid.
44. Westermeyer, *Te Deum,* 26.
46. Ibid., 27.
47. Schaff, *Creeds of Christendom,* 3:10.
48. Leaver, "Music and Lutheranism," 38.
49. Ibid.
50. Ibid.
51. Ibid.
52. Boyd, *Bach,* 78.
53. Leisinger, *Bach in Leipzig,* 12.
54. Bettmann, *Bach,* 125.
55. David and Mendel, *New Bach Reader,* 151–52.
56. Bettmann, *Bach,* 123.
57. David and Mendel, *New Bach Reader,* 149.
58. Ibid., 151.
59. Bettmann, *Bach,* 126.
60. David and Mendel, *New Bach Reader,* 204.
61. Wolff, *Bach,* 454.
62. Miles, *Bach,* 162.
63. Ibid.
64. Bettmann, *Bach,* 14.
65. Ibid., 15.
66. Ibid., 14.
67. Ibid., 16.
68. Butt, "Historical Perspective and Introduction," 2.
69. Boyd, *Bach,* 168.
70. Ibid.
71. Ibid.
72. Miles, *Bach,* 122.
73. Wolff, *Bach,* 6.
74. Dickinson, *Music in the History of the Western Church,* 306–7.
75. Wolff, *Bach,* 19–20.
76. Miles, *Bach,* 71.
77. Viladesau, *Theology and the Arts,* 44.
78. Unger, *Handbook to Bach's Sacred Cantata Texts.*
79. Wolff, *Bach,* 449.
80. Miles, *Bach,* 160–61.
81. Wolff, *Bach,* 450.
82. Miles, *Bach,* 161.
83. Viladesau, *Theology and the Arts,* 45.
84. Wright, "Resurrection," 203.

85. Dickinson, *Music in the History of the Western Church,* 301.

86. Leisinger, *Bach in Leipzig,* 15.

87. Dickinson, *Music in the History of the Western Church,* 301.

88. Ibid., 304.

89. David and Mendel, *New Bach Reader,* 17.

90. Ibid., 18.

91. Ibid.

92. Chafe, *Tonal Allegory,* 227.

93. Ibid., 227–28.

94. Stapert, *My Only Comfort,* 5.

95. Ibid., 6.

96. Bettmann, *Bach,* 128.

97. Stapert, *My Only Comfort,* 4–5.

98. Marissen, *Social and Religious Designs,* 116–17.

99. Leaver, *Bach and Scripture,* 121–22.

100. Wolff, *Bach,* 312.

101. David and Mendel, *New Bach Reader,* 118.

102. Wolff, *Bach,* 313.

103. Marissen, *Social and Religious Designs,* 117.

104. Ibid.

105. Leaver, "Mature Vocal Works," 96.

106. Grout, *History of Western Music,* 420.

107. David and Mendel, *New Bach Reader,* 196.

108. Ibid., 231.

109. Ibid., 231–32.

110. Boyd, *Bach,* 131.

111. Wolff, *Bach,* 350.

112. David and Mendel, *New Bach Reader,* 174.

113. Ibid., 172–85, 189–96.

114. Stravinsky, *Poetics of Music,* 63.

115. Peters, *Christian Imagination,* 45.

116. Ibid.

117. Stravinsky, *Poetics of Music,* 65.

118. Wolff, *Bach,* 93.

119. David and Mendel, *New Bach Reader,* 397.

120. Wolff, *Bach,* 170–71.

121. Boyd, *Bach,* 3.

122. Dickinson, *Music in the History of the Western Church,* 287–88.

123. Stapert, *My Only Comfort,* 18.

124. Bettmann, *Bach,* 177.

125. Ibid.

126. Schonberg, *Lives of the Great Composers,* 46.

127. David and Mendel, *New Bach Reader,* 441.

128. Ibid.

129. Wolff, *Bach,* 174.

130. Ibid.

131. Bettmann, *Bach,* 44.

132. Wolff, *Bach,* 7.

133. Ibid., 335.

134. Boyd, *Bach,* 206.

135. Wolff, *Bach,* 310.

136. Ibid., 5.

137. Bettmann, *Bach,* 129.

138. Viladesau, *Theology and the Arts,* 69.

139. Bettmann, *Bach,* 79.

140. David and Mendel, *New Bach Reader,* 396–97.

141. Bettmann, *Bach,* 22.

142. Miles, *Bach,* 37.

143. David and Mendel, *New Bach Reader,* 459.

144. Wolff, *Bach,* 9.

145. Ibid., 327.

146. Leisinger, *Bach in Leipzig,* 7.

147. Daw, "Bach as Teacher and Model," 196.

148. Leisinger, *Bach in Leipzig,* 66.

149. Miles, 37.

150. David and Mendel, *New Bach Reader,* 97–98.

151. Ibid., 80.

152. Ibid., 129.

153. Daw, "Bach as Teacher and Model," 201.

154. Wolff, *Bach,* 309.

155. David and Mendel, *New Bach Reader,* 475–76.

156. Ibid., 17.

157. Bettmann, *Bach,* 41.

158. David and Mendel, *New Bach Reader,* 474.

159. Ibid., 334.

160. Butt, "Bach's Metaphysics of Music," 58.

161. Ibid., 57.

162. Wolff, *Bach,* 339.

163. Grout, *History of Western Music,* 435.

164. Dickinson, *Music in the History of the Western Church,* 283.

165. Grout, *History of Western Music,* 420.

166. Bettmann, *Bach,* 188.

167. David and Mendel, *New Bach Reader,* 411.

168. Grout, *History of Western Music,* 432.

169. Dickinson, *Music in the History of the Western Church,* 314.

170. Ibid., 305.

171. Schonberg, *Lives of the Great Composers,* 48.

172. Dickinson, *Music in the History of the Western Church,* 296.

173. Grout, *History of Western Music,* 420.

174. Bettmann, *Bach,* 189.

175. Schonberg, *Lives of the Great Composers,* 48.

176. Boyd, *Bach,* 159.

177. Stapert, *My Only Comfort,* 33.

178. Ibid.

179. Ibid., 34.

180. Leaver, "The Mature Vocal Works," 107.

181. Stapert, *My Only Comfort,* 37.

182. Jordan, "The Lutheran Chorale, 36.

183. Stapert, *My Only Comfort,* 37.

184. Ibid., 136.

185. Jordan, "The Lutheran Chorale," 37.

186. Boyd, *Bach,* 159.

187. Grout, *History of Western Music,* 433.

188. David and Mendel, *New Bach Reader,* 461.

189. Bettmann, *Bach,* 100.

190. Ibid., 101.

191. David and Mendel, *New Bach Reader,* 208–9.

192. Ibid., 209.

193. Bettmann, *Bach,* 102.

194. David and Mendel, *New Bach Reader,* 459.

195. Miles, *Bach,* 4–5.

196. Bettmann, *Bach,* 65–66.

197. Miles, *Bach,* 43.

198. Bettmann, *Bach,* 155.

199. David and Mendel, *New Bach Reader,* 152.

200. Wolff, *Bach,* 219.

201. Ibid.

202. David and Mendel, *New Bach Reader,* 200.

203. Ibid., 202.

204. Ibid., 422.

205. Miles, *Bach,* 118.

206. Bettmann, *Bach,* 21.

207. Ibid.

208. Ibid., 112.

209. Ibid., 39.

210. Boyd, *Bach,* 162–163.

211. Ibid., 162.

212. Miles, *Bach,* 118.

213. Leisinger, *Bach in Leipzig,* 22.

214. Miles, *Bach,* 104.

215. Bettmann, *Bach,* 21.

216. Leisinger, *Bach in Leipzig,* 23.

217. Wolff, *Bach,* 406.

218. David and Mendel, *New Bach Reader,* 216.

219. Wolff, *Bach,* 408.
220. David and Mendel, *New Bach Reader,* 400.
221. Wolff, 408.
222. David and Mendel, *New Bach Reader,* 366.
223. Ibid., 152.
224. Wolff, *Bach,* 408.
225. David and Mendel, *New Bach Reader,* 251–53.
226. Wolff, *Bach,* 409.
227. David and Mendel, *New Bach Reader,* 438.
228. Ibid., 418.
229. Ibid., 420–21.
230. Ibid., 436.
231. Ibid., 446.
232. Ibid., 478.
233. Miles, *Bach,* 19.
234. Bettmann, *Bach,* 80.
235. Ibid., 82–84.
236. Leisinger, *Bach in Leipzig,* 89.
237. Grout, *History of Western Music,* 429.
238. Daw, "Bach as Teacher and Model," 196.
239. Wolff, *Bach,* 351–55.
240. Ibid., 360.
241. Dickinson, *Music in the History of the Western Church,* 286.
242. Stapert, *My Only Comfort,* 24.
243. Boyd, *Bach,* 122.
244. Schonberg, *Lives of the Great Composers,* 45.
245. Dickinson, *Music in the History of the Western Church,* 314–15.
246. Schonberg, *Lives of the Great Composers,* 48.
247. Miles, *Bach,* 61.
248. David and Mendel, *New Bach Reader,* 434.
249. Wolff, *Bach,* 413.
250. David and Mendel, *New Bach Reader,* 365–66.
251. Wolff, *Bach,* 414.
252. Ibid., 229.
253. Ibid.
254. Ibid., 8.
255. Ferguson, *History of Musical Thought,* 310.
256. David and Mendel, *New Bach Reader,* 375.
257. Ibid., 501.
258. Ibid.
259. Bettmann, *Bach,* 82–83.
260. Ibid., 83.
261. Ferguson, *History of Musical Thought,* 310.
262. Ibid.
263. Bettmann, *Bach,* 83.
264. Stapert, *My Only Comfort,* 4–5.
265. Miles, *Bach,* 31.

266. Bettmann, *Bach,* 171.
267. Ibid., 175.
268. Ibid., 174.
269. Ibid., 176–77.
270. Butt, "Historical Prospective and Introduction," 3.
271. Stapert, *My Only Comfort,* 5.
272. Bettmann, *Bach,* 186.
273. David and Mendel, *New Bach Reader,* 16.
274. Ibid.
275. Ibid., 17.
276. Leaver, "Mature Vocal Works," 96.
277. Boyd, *Bach,* 179.

PART 3: THE LEGACY OF JOHANN SEBASTIAN BACH

1. Butt, "Historical Perspective and Introduction," 2.
2. David and Mendel, *New Bach Reader,* 448.
3. Grout, *History of Western Music,* 435.
4. Viladesau, *Theology and the Arts,* 45.

Selected Bibliography

Bettmann, Otto L. *Johann Sebastian Bach: As His World Knew Him.* New York: Carol Publishing Group, 1995.

Blume, Friedrich. "Outline of a New Picture of Bach." *Music and Letters* 44 (1963): 219–20.

Boyd, Malcolm. *Bach.* 3rd edition. New York: Oxford University Press, 2000.

———. "The Bach Family." In *The Cambridge Companion to Bach,* edited by John Butt. Cambridge: Cambridge University Press, 2000.

Butt, John. "Bach's Metaphysics of Music." In *The Cambridge Companion to Bach,* edited by John Butt. Cambridge: Cambridge University Press, 2000.

———. "Historical Perspective and Introduction." In *The Sacred Choral Music of J. S. Bach: A Handbook,* edited by John Butt. Brewster, MA: Paraclete Press, 1997.

Chafe, Eric. *Tonal Allegory in the Vocal Music of J. S. Bach.* Berkeley and Los Angeles: University of California Press, 1991.

David, Hans T., and Arthur Mendel, eds. *The New Bach Reader: A Life of Johann Sebastian Bach in Letters and Documents.* Revised and enlarged by Christoph Wolff. New York: Norton, 1998.

Daw, Stephan. "Bach as Teacher and Model." In *The Cambridge Companion to Bach,* edited by John Butt. Cambridge: Cambridge University Press, 1997.

Dickinson, Edward. *Music in the History of the Western Church.* New York: Scribner's, 1902.

Ferguson, Donald N. *A History of Musical Thought.* 3rd ed. New York: Appleton-Century-Crofts, 1959.

Grout, Donald Jay. *A History of Western Music.* 3rd ed. New York: Norton, 1980.

Jordan, James E., Jr. "The Lutheran Chorale: A Key to the Interpretation of Bach's Choral Music." In *The Sacred Choral Music of J. S. Bach: A Handbook,* edited by John Butt. Brewster, MA: Paraclete Press, 1997.

Leaver, Robin A. *J. S. Bach and Scripture.* St. Louis: Concordia Publishing House, 1986.

———. "The Mature Vocal Works and Their Theological and Liturgical Context." In *The Cambridge Companion to Bach,* edited by John Butt. Cambridge: Cambridge University Press, 2000.

———. "Music and Lutheranism." In *The Cambridge Companion to Bach,* edited by John Butt. Cambridge: Cambridge University Press, 2000.

Leisinger, Ulrich. *Bach in Leipzig.* Berlin: Die Deutsche Bibliothek, 2000.

Marissen, Michael. *The Social and Religious Designs of J. S. Bach's Brandenburg Concertos.* Princeton, NJ: Princeton University Press, 1995.

Miles, Russell H. *Johann Sebastian Bach: An Introduction to His Life and Music.* Englewood Cliffs, NJ: Prentice-Hall, 1962.

Peters, Thomas C. *The Christian Imagination: G. K. Chesterton on the Arts.* San Francisco: Ignatius Press, 2000.

Schaff, Philip, ed. *The Creeds of Christendom.* Revised by David S. Schaff. Grand Rapids. MI: Baker Books, 1996.

Schonberg, Harold C. *The Lives of the Great Composers.* 3rd ed. New York: Norton, 1997.

Shannon, Martin. "'Soli Deo Gloria.'" In *The Sacred Choral Music of J. S. Bach: A Handbook,* edited by John Butt. Brewster, MA: Paraclete Press, 1997.

Spitta, Philipp. *Johann Sebastian Bach.* Translated by Clara Bell and J. A. Fuller-Maitland. 3 vols. New York: Dover, 1951.

Stapert, Calvin R. *My Only Comfort: Death, Deliverance, and Discipleship in the Music of Bach.* Grand Rapids, MI: Eerdmans, 2000.

Stravinsky, Igor. *The Poetics of Music in the Form of Six Lessons.* Cambridge, MA: Harvard University Press, 1970.

Unger, Melvin P. *Handbook to Bach's Sacred Cantata Texts.* Lanham, MD: Scarecrow Press, 1996.

Viladesau, Richard. *Theology and the Arts: Encountering God through Music, Art and Rhetoric.* New York: Paulist Press, 2000.

Westermeyer, Peter. *Te Deum: The Church and Music.* Minneapolis: Fortress Press, 1989.

Wolff, Christoph. *Johann Sebastian Bach: The Learned Musician.* New York: Norton, 2000.

Wright, N. T. "Resurrection: From Theology to Music and Back Again." In *Sounding the Depths: Theology Through the Arts.* Edited by Jeremy Begbie. London: SCM Press, 2002.

INDEX

Agricola, Johann Friedrich, 213
Altnickol, Johann Christoph, 87,
    100–101
Arnstadt, Germany, 4, 8, 12, 15,
    25–27, 29–34, 111, 165, 188
Augsburg Confession, 112, 128
Augustine, 67, 184

Bach, Ambrosius, 6, 195, 200
Bach, Anna Magdalena Wülken,
    58, 64, 85, 101–2, 133, 139,
    189–191, 199
Bach, Barbara Margaretha, 12, 64,
    200
Bach, Carl Philipp Emanuel, 3, 65,
    85, 87–88, 92, 98, 101–2,
    119–21, 124, 159, 164, 170,
    195, 200–201, 204, 219
Bach, Caspar, 27
Bach, Christiana Sophia Henrietta,
    64, 85
Bach, Elisabeth Juliana Friederica,
    87
Bach, Elisabeth Lämmerhirt, 3, 6
Bach, Friedelena Margaretha, 64,
    200
Bach, Gottfried Heinrich, 101
Bach, Heinrich, 27
Bach, Johann Ambrosius, 6
Bach, Johann Christian, 87, 101–2

Bach, Johann Christoph Friedrich,
    87, 102
Bach, Johann Christoph, 11, 27
Bach, Johann Elias, 83, 153,
    190–91, 201
Bach, Johann Ernst, 31
Bach, Johann Friedrich, 37
Bach, Johann Gottfried Bernhard,
    24, 37, 85, 87, 194–95
Bach, Johann Günther, 12
Bach, Johann Jacob, 9
Bach, Johanna Dorothea Vonhoff,
    16
Back, Johanna Juditha, 9
Bach, Johannes Jonas, 9
Bach, Leopold Augustus, 55
Bach, Magdalena, 58, 60, 64, 85,
    101–2, 133, 139, 189–91, 199
Bach, Maria Salome, 9, 13
Bach, Regina Susanna, 193
Bach, Tobias Friedrich, 16
Bach, Veit, 3, 102
Bach, Wilhelm Friedemann, 80,
    225
Balthasar, Johann, 9
Baron, Jacob, 132
Beethoven, Ludwig van, 103, 167,
    196, 219
Berlin, Germany, 8, 55–56, 170
Bernstein, Leonard, 186

Bettmann, Otto, 132, 136, 166, 169, 182, 193, 196, 208
Biggs, E. Power, 140
Bismarck, Otto, 218
Blume, Friedrich, 115
Böhm, Georg, 22
Book of Concord, 117, 129
Boyd, Malcolm, 136, 187, 227
Brahms, Johannes, 208, 218–19
Brandenburg Concertos, 58, 61–62, 197
Brueghel, Pieter, 66
Butt, John, 136, 178, 222
Buxtehude, Dietrich, 29

Calov[ius] Bible), 112, 116, 149
Catherine Winkworth, 220
Chafe, Eric, 146
Chesterton, G. K., 158
Collegium Musicum, 71, 88, 90, 98, 197, 210, 217
Corelli, Archangel, 219
Countess of Schwarzburg, 26
Couperin, François, 219
Crämer, C. F., 181

Daw, Stephan, 173
Desprez, Josquin, 219
Dickinson, Edward, 161, 210–11
Diet of Worms, 6
Drese, Johann Wilhelm, 43, 49, 52–53
Drese, Samuel, 42–43, 49, 52
Duke Christian, 42
Duke Ernst Augustus, 51–52
Duke of Saxe-Weissenfels, 24

Duke Wilhelm Ernst, 36, 40–43, 51–53

Eilmer, Georg, 35
Emperor Joseph, 35
Erdmann, Georg, 18, 72, 88, 132, 202
Ernesti, Johann August, 81, 136
Ernesti, Johann Heinrich, 77

Ferguson, Donald, 119
Forkel, Johann Nikolaus, xx, xxviii, 22, 39, 47, 92, 110, 113, 119, 121, 123, 125, 165, 177, 195, 204–6, 212, 235
Friedrich August I, 79, 150
Friedrich August II, 79
Friedrich Wilhelm I, 56
Friedrich, Tobias, 16

Gelatt, Roland, 199
Georgenkirche, 3
Gerlach, Carl Gotthelf, 71
German Reformation, 5
Gesner, Johann Mattias, 78
Geysersbach, Johann Heinrich, 28
Görner, Johann Gottlieb, 71, 150–51
Graupner, Johann Christoph, 59
Grout, Donald Jay, 50, 70, 179–80, 187, 236

Handel, George Frideric, 30, 58, 182, 218
Harrer, Gottlob, 97
Herder, Elias, 18

Kepler, Johannes, 168
Kretzschmar, Hermann, 139
Kuhnau, Johann, 197

Leaver, Robin, 112, 117, 152, 227
Leipzig, Germany, 8, 16, 54, 56,
    59–60, 62, 64–67, 70–73, 80,
    85–88, 90, 97, 99, 113, 116,
    124, 128–29, 131–33, 135–36,
    140, 144–45, 149–51, 153,
    155, 173, 177, 185, 189, 191,
    193–97, 202, 209, 211, 217,
    221
Leipzig, University of, 87, 90, 113,
    116
Luther, Martin, 3, 5, 66, 75, 93,
    108, 112, 116

Marchand, Louis, 53, 120
Marissen, Michael, 149
Marpurg, Freidrich Wilhelm, 216
Melanchthon, Philipp, 128
Mendelssohn, Felix, 103, 217,
    219, 222, 224
Miles, Russell, 81, 133, 196, 212
Mizler, Lorenz Christoph, 90–91,
    96, 169
Mozart, Wolfgang Amadeus, 14,
    103, 219
Mühlhausen, Germany, 8, 31,
    33–38, 40, 53, 87, 200, 221

Nicene Creed, 94

Orhdruf, Germany, 15–16, 18
Ovid, 198

Pachelbel, Johann, 9, 15, 219
Palestrina, Giovanni Pierluigi da,
    219
Parry, C. Hubert H., 196
Peters, Thomas C., 158
Pitschel, Theodor Leberecht, 177
Pope Leo, 184
Potsdam, Germany, 87, 92–93
Prince Johann Ernst, 51
Prince Leopold of Anhalt-Cöthen-
    Saxe, 52, 57, 101
Prince of Saxe-Weissenfels, 80
Princess Elenore Wilhelmine, 52
Princess Gisela Agnes, 55

Radigast, Samuel, 220
Raphael, 66
Reinken, Johann Adam, 22
Rembrandt van Rijn, 66, 142
Richter, Johann Christoph, 66

Saxe-Weissenfels, Duke of, 24, 80
Saxe-Weissenfels, Germany, 42
Saxony, Germany, 65, 79, 92, 101
Scheib, Adolf, 124
Schneider, Johann, 71
Schonberg, Harold, 211
Schubart, Johann Martin, 53
Schumann, Robert, 20, 217, 219
Schwarzburg-Arnstadt, Germany,
    27
Schweinfurt, Germany, 8
Shannon, Martin, 117
Shostakovich, Dimitri, 219
Silbermann, Gottfried, 125–26,
    213

Sorge, G. A., 121
Spitta, Philipp, 36
St. Blasius, 33–37
St. Boniface Church, 26
St. Boniface, 15
St. Catherine, 22
St. George Latin School, 11
St. George, 3, 6–7, 11–12
St. Jacob, 24
St. John Passion, 70, 73, 89, 101, 181
St. Mary, 29, 34–35, 37
St. Matthew Passion, 70, 73, 82, 103, 181, 184–87, 221–22
St. Nicholas Church, 69, 71, 98, 124, 150
St. Paul, 71
St. Sophia, 26, 80
St. Thomas Church (Thomskirche), 67, 132, 151
Stapert, Calvin, 76, 147, 162, 185, 221
Stravinsky, Igor, 157–58, 219
Sweelinck, Jan Pieterszon, 23

Telemann, Georg Philipp, 30, 52, 59, 131, 219
Thuringian Forest, 15, 26

Tinctoris, Johannes, 224
Tolkien, J. R. R., 158

University of Jena, 195
University of Leipzig, 87, 90, 113, 116

Venice, Italy, 56
Vienna, Austria, 33, 56
Viladesau, Richard, 140
Vivaldi, Antonio, 50–51, 159, 165, 219

Wagner, Richard, 218–19
Walton, William, 219
Wartburg Castle, 6
Wiemar, Germany, 165
Wilhelmsburg, Germany, 40–41
Winckler, Gottfried, 66
Winkworth, Catherine, 220
Wolff, Christoph, 7, 14, 43, 122, 124, 138, 165–66, 172, 175, 203, 214
Worms, Diet of, 6

Zimmermann's Coffeehouse, 71, 195, 197–98, 210, 217